BAFFINS
BAY

ARCTICK LAND

NEW NORTH
WALES

NEW SOUTH
WALES

HUDSONS BAY

TERRA
LABRADOR

NEW
BRITAIN

Hudsons Charles Straits

NEW
FOUND
LAND

The Main
Bank

Falls
Bank

ract of Land
of Wild Bulls

L. PISCOUTAGAMI

NEW FRANCE

LAKE SUPERIOR

LAKE HURONS

LAKE ERIE

PENN

MARY
IRGI
NI

CapeCod

ENGLISH EMPIRE

Bermudes als
Sommer Islands

THE GO
B
A
MEX

TI N D I A N

SEA
CARIBY
ISLANDS

PAIN

· VOICES ·
from
COLONIAL AMERICA

SOUTH CAROLINA

1540 – 1776

ROBIN DOAK
WITH
ROBERT OLWELL, PH.D., CONSULTANT

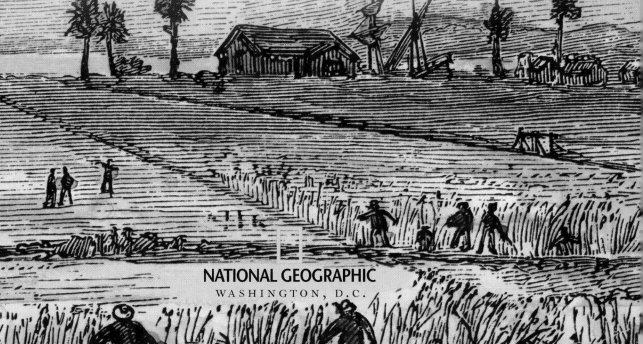

NATIONAL GEOGRAPHIC
WASHINGTON, D.C.

John M. Fahey, Jr., *President and Chief Executive Officer*
Gilbert M. Grosvenor, *Chairman of the Board*
Nina D. Hoffman, *Executive Vice President, President, Book Publishing Group*

STAFF FOR THIS BOOK

Nancy Laties Feresten, *Vice President, Editor-in-Chief of Children's Books*
Amy Shields, *Executive Editor, Children's Books*
Suzanne Patrick Fonda, *Project Editor*
Robert D. Johnston, Ph.D., *Associate Professor and Director, Teaching of History Program University of Illinois at Chicago, Series Editor*
Bea Jackson, *Director of Illustration and Design, Children's Books*
Jean Cantu, *Illustrations Specialist*
Carl Mehler, *Director of Maps*
Justin Morrill, *The M Factory, Inc., Map Research, Design, and Production*
Rebecca Baines, *Editorial Assistant*
Jennifer Thornton, *Managing Editor*
Connie D. Binder, *Indexer*
R. Gary Colbert, *Production Director*
Lewis R. Bassford, *Production Manager*
Nicole Elliott and Maryclare Tracy, *Manufacturing Managers*

Voices from Colonial South Carolina was prepared by
CREATIVE MEDIA APPLICATIONS, INC.

Robin Doak, *Writer*
Fabia Wargin Design, Inc., *Design and Production*
Susan Madoff, *Editor*
Laurie Lieb, *Copyeditor*
Cynthia Joyce, *Image Researcher*

Body text is set in Deepdene, sidebars are Caslon 337 Oldstyle, and display type is Cochin Archaic Bold.

Library of Congress Cataloging in Publication Data
Doak, Robin S. (Robin Santos), 1963–
   South Carolina, 1540–1776 / by Robin Doak.
      p. cm. — (Voices from colonial America)
   Includes bibliographical references.
   ISBN 978-1-4263-0066-0 (trade)
   ISBN 978-1-4263-0067-7 (library)
   1. South Carolina—History—Colonial period, ca. 1600-1775—Juvenile literature. I. Title.
   F272.D63 2007
   975.7'02—dc22
                                    2007003120

Printed in Belgium

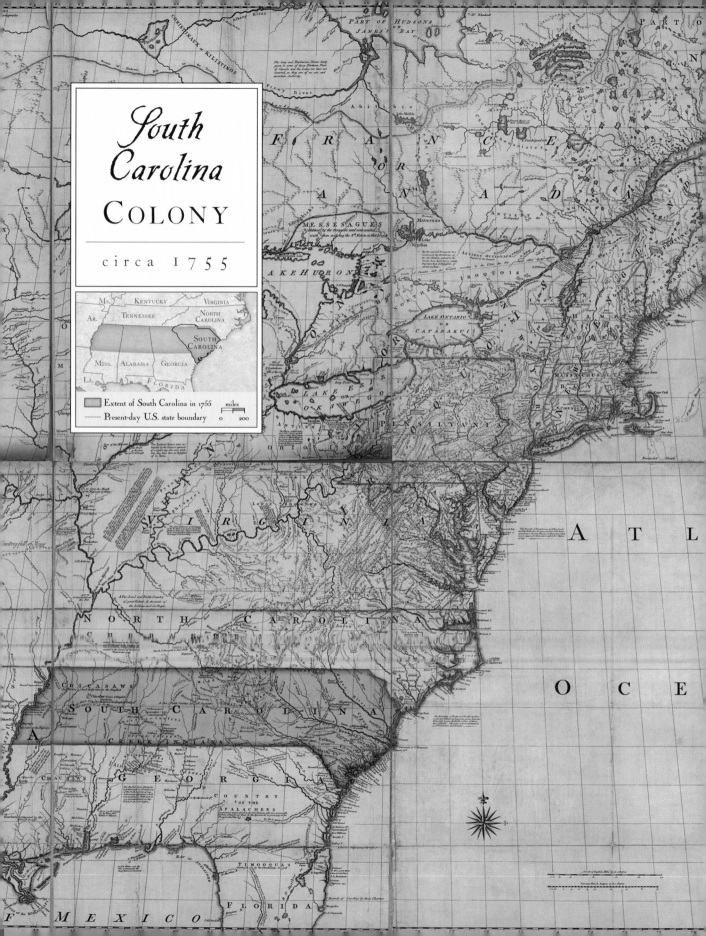

INTRODUCTION

by

Robert Olwell, Ph.D.

A settler pulls his skiff ashore in front of his cabin along
a South Carolina waterway.

The place we now call South Carolina was first settled in
1670 by the English, who named the region "Carolina," after
their king. In 1719, when the vast Carolina grant was divided
into two, the colony known as South Carolina was born.

Many traces of South Carolina's colonial past remain
today. Place-names such as Ashepoo, Edisto, Kiawah, and
Wappoo recall the native peoples who lived on the coast
when the Europeans first appeared. In Charleston, historic
buildings and cobbled streets survive from the days when

OPPOSITE: This historical map, created by John Mitchell in 1755, has been
colorized for this book to emphasize the boundaries of the South Carolina
colony. The inset map shows the state's present-day boundaries for comparison.

it was among the largest and richest cities in all of the Colonies. On the islands or tidal rivers near the coast, miles of surviving banks and ditches offer silent testimony to the Herculean labors of the generations of enslaved Africans and their descendants who transformed virgin swampland into rice fields.

The history of colonial South Carolina is the story of how three peoples—Native Americans, Europeans, and Africans—struggled alongside and against each other to build a new society or to preserve or recreate an ancient way of life.

Francisco Chicora, an Indian captured and taken to Spain, returned to help his people resist Spanish conquest. Eliza Lucas Pinckney, a young woman left in charge of a plantation, helped developed indigo as a profitable new crop for the colony, and John Locke's "Fundamental Constitutions of Carolina" was a blueprint for the infant colony and an influential argument for a tie between private property and political rights.

The seal of South Carolina prior to the American Revolution featured a Palmetto tree, an important natural resource for early settlers.

In the 18th century, people who were bought and sold as slaves were the most valuable form of property in the colony. In South Carolina, alone among the 13 original colonies, enslaved Africans and their descendents made up most of the population. Despite their shackles, these

Africans contributed greatly to the colony. They provided the original seed and knowledge for the cultivation of rice, South Carolina's major export. Among themselves, slaves created the Gullah language, a mixture of African and English that can still be heard in parts of the rural low-country. Africans also pulled against their chains. In 1739, Jemmy, a native of Angola in Africa, led the largest slave revolt in all of colonial American history.

South Carolina played a key role in the American Revolution. South Carolinians were the first Americans to declare independence from Britain, more than three months before July 4, 1776. No other state was the scene of more battles. The Revolution in South Carolina was truly a civil war. The conflict pit Patriot against Tory, lowcountry against backcountry, and slave against master. Many slaves saw in the disorders of war an opportunity to gain their own liberty by escaping to (and fighting for) the British. Thomas Jeremiah, a free black fisherman, was convicted and hanged for calling upon blacks to join the king's troops.

The British defeat at Cowpens in early 1781 was the first step on the road that would lead to Yorktown and the victory that would bring America's independence.

In this volume of *Voices of Colonial America*, readers will hear from some of the key players in South Carolina's history and see how the decisions they faced and the choices they made not only created the world they lived in but helped shape the present.

CHAPTER ONE

Early Exploration

EXPLORERS FROM SPAIN AND FRANCE *lay claim to what will become South Carolina as early as 1521, but neither empire establishes a permanent settlement in the region.*

 outh Carolina, settled in 1670, was the first of England's southern colonies (North Carolina, South Carolina, and Georgia) to be founded. At first, North Carolina and South Carolina were part of the same colony, called simply Carolina. This volume deals with the events of the region that is now known as South Carolina.

Although Charles Town, the first permanent settlement in South Carolina, was established by English

OPPOSITE: An engraving by Theodore de Bry of Jean Ribault and his men (on the island, left and center) in the region they claimed for France and named Charlesfort.

colonists, both Spain and France had earlier claims to the region. In 1521, nearly 150 years before the English settlers arrived, Spanish trader Francisco Gordillo became the first European to explore the South Carolina region. Gordillo and his crew set sail from the Spanish colony of Santo Domingo on the Caribbean island of Hispaniola. They traveled along the coasts of what are now Florida, South Carolina, North Carolina, Georgia, and Virginia before turning back. In Florida, Gordillo and another captain kidnapped about 150 native people to work as slaves in Spain's New World colonies in the Caribbean, Central America, Mexico, and South America.

RELOCATING A SPANISH SETTLEMENT

FOR MANY YEARS, HISTORIANS BELIEVED THAT THE FIRST European settlement in South Carolina was San Miguel de Gualdape, a Spanish outpost founded in 1526 by Lucas Vásquez de Ayllón. The short-lived colony was believed to have been founded somewhere along the Carolina coast. But after rereading contemporary Spanish accounts in an effort to pinpoint the settlement's exact location, historians and archaeologists now believe that San Miguel was more likely on St. Catherines Island off the coast of Georgia.

conquistador—a
Spanish soldier who
explored the Americas
in the 1500s

In 1540, Spanish conquistador
Hernando de Soto explored part of South
Carolina. De Soto had set off from Florida
the year before on an expedition through the
southeastern region of what is now the United States. De
Soto and his party of about 600 soldiers were looking for
gold, precious gems, and other valuables. The men followed native pathways through Florida into southwest
Georgia and northwestern South Carolina. De Soto turned
back when he reached the foothills of the Blue Ridge
Mountains there. The Blue Ridge Mountains, a section of
the Appalachian Mountains, stretch from West Virginia
into northern Georgia.

During his journey, de Soto came into contact with the
native people who lived in the region. He forced the
natives to serve as guides and to carry equipment during the
journey. De Soto's men also stole native food supplies and
spread European diseases such as smallpox and plague. The
native population had never before been
exposed to these sicknesses and therefore
had no natural immunity to them. These and
other diseases brought by future explorers
would eventually cause a serious decline in the native population in South Carolina. According to one historian, the
population of Indian tribes along the South Carolina coast
might have been reduced *to the extent of decimation [destruc-
tion]* by 1670.

plague—a deadly,
contagious disease
caused by bacteria

THE FIRST PEOPLE

Native Americans had lived in the South Carolina region for more than 10,000 years before the Spanish arrived. By the early 1500s, as many as 30 tribes lived in the region now known as South Carolina. The most important of these tribes were the Cherokee in the northwest, the Catawba in the north, and the Yamassee in the southeast.

The Cherokee were the largest of the Carolina tribes. When the first Europeans arrived, there were about 200 Cherokee villages in the area. The Cherokee were farmers and hunters who lived in circular huts made with branches, bark, and mud. The men of a village cleared the land of trees, while the women planted and tended the crops. They grew corn, beans, squash, and pumpkins, along with a little tobacco.

Although they lived in the mountainous northwest, the Cherokee often ventured farther south to hunt. The forests of South Carolina were home to a wide variety of animals that were good for eating, including rabbit and deer. Deer meat was a good source of protein, and the Cherokee and other tribes used deerskins to make clothing. Natives also ate wild duck, quail, and turkey.

Along South Carolina's coast and rivers, Indians supplemented their diet with fish caught with nets woven from grass and wood fibers, fishing spears, or fishing rods with bone fishhooks. Shellfish such as clams and oysters were also eaten. Other sources of food were edible roots, plants, nuts, and berries.

The Cherokee traveled to other parts of southeastern America to wage war against other tribes, especially the Catawba to the east and the Creek tribes to the south. Long before Europeans settled the region, the Cherokee drove the Creek out of South Carolina, across the Savannah River and into present-day Georgia. In the future, this constant friction between the tribes in the region would help the colonists take over tribal lands.

Creek Indians in South Carolina are shown in their village tending the fire, cooking, and socializing.

FRENCH AND SPANISH SETTLEMENTS

Despite early Spanish exploration, the first people to try to settle South Carolina were French. In February 1562, naval officer Jean Ribault and a group of about 150 men set sail in two ships for the New World. Ribault and most of the travelers were Huguenots, Protestants who followed the teachings of French religious scholar John Calvin. Living in France, a Roman Catholic country, the Huguenots were often the victims of persecution. Ribault hoped to found a settlement where he and his friends could freely practice their religion.

Huguenot—a Protestant who followed the teachings of pastor John Calvin

In April, the ships made landfall in Florida, which Ribault claimed for France. However, they decided that this was too close to Spain's Catholic colonies in the Caribbean, and they continued sailing north. In May, they landed on an island off the coast of Carolina, probably present-day Parris Island. Ribault later called the harbor *"the greatest and fairest of the greatest havens of the world."* Here, the French were greeted by Indians who offered the strangers food.

After some exploration, Ribault decided that this place was suitable for a settlement. The explorer was impressed with the land and its climate. He believed that there was plenty of game and fish to support a new colony. In the report of his expedition, written two years later, Ribault wrote, "It is one of the most fruitful countries that ever was seen, and where nothing lacketh, and also as good as can be found in other places." His crew built a fortress, which they named Charlesfort.

In June, Ribault set sail for France for more supplies, leaving 30 men behind. Ribault left food and other supplies for the first French settlers in the region. He promised to return as soon as possible with more colonists and supplies for the new colony. When Ribault returned to France, however, the country was in the midst of a civil war between Protestants and Catholics. Ribault fled to England, where he hoped to obtain assistance from Queen Elizabeth I. Although she promised assistance, Ribault was suspected of spying and thrown into prison.

The men Ribault had left behind in Charlesfort were not prepared for the hardships of living in the New World. Their food ran out quickly so they had to rely completely on the Indians for supplies, which were not enough to sustain the men. With morale declining, several of the men mutinied, or rebelled, and murdered the colony's leader, Albert de la Pierra. In the fall of 1562, the remaining colonists built a small boat and set sail for France— without any maps or navigational equipment. After weeks at sea, those still surviving resorted to killing and eating one of their shipmates to stay alive. They were eventually saved after being spotted by an English ship off the coast of England.

In 1565, Ribault was released from prison and returned to France. He soon set sail for the New World again. This time his mission was to aid the newly established Huguenot settlement of Fort Caroline (established by René Goulaine de Laudonniére) on the St. Johns River in Florida. Ribault left with three ships and 600 people.

During this time, the Spaniards' interest in "their" territory in South Carolina resurfaced. Spanish troops, under the command of Pedro Menéndez de Avilés, were ordered to find any colonies along the coast and *"cast them out by the best means that seems to you possible."* When word of this plan reached Ribault, he sailed past the mouth of the St. Johns River to St. Augustine, where Menéndez's men were stationed, intending to wipe them out. Meanwhile, Spanish troops traveled overland and massacred the settlers at Fort Caroline. Ribault and his men met with death shortly thereafter when their ships were destroyed in a hurricane, leaving them stranded on the coast of St. Augustine. It did not take long for Menéndez's troops to find and kill them. When Menéndez reported the death of Ribault to King Philip II of Spain, he wrote, *"I think it a great good fortune that this man be dead, for the King of France could accomplish more with him and fifty thousand ducats than with other men and five hundred thousand ducats; and he could do more in one year than another in ten."*

In 1566, Menéndez founded the Spanish settlement of Santa Elena on the southern end of Parris Island. Santa Elena was very close to the former site of Charlesfort. The new arrivals burned the French huts and took down the stone marker that Ribault had erected to claim the region for France.

Menéndez sent parties of men into the interior to explore the land that is now South Carolina. As they advanced deeper into the region, they built small garrisons to cement Spain's claim to the land. They also met native people as they traveled. But instead of trying to make allies of the Indians, the Spaniards attacked them, forcing some to work as slaves. Others died from the diseases these intruders brought with them. Later, when the English arrived, these Indians would remember their treatment at the hands of the Spaniards.

Once the Spanish had returned to the coastline, the native people quickly burned down their garrisons. Later, they burned down the fortress of Santa Elena too, putting an end to the Spanish presence in South Carolina.

For now, the Europeans were gone. They would not return for nearly a century and a half. ✺

This ceramic goblet (drinking vessel), discovered on Parris Island, dates back to the late 1500s when the Spanish inhabited the region. It is believed to be the oldest piece of European pottery found in the United States.

CHAPTER TWO

The English Arrive

The English settle Carolina in 1669 with immigrants arriving from the British Isles and Barbados, an island in the West Indies. Early settlers form cooperative relationships with Native Americans.

he English traced their claims to Carolina back to a voyage that explorer John Cabot had made to North America in 1497. Cabot is believed to have landed in present-day Newfoundland, Canada, and explored some of the coastline in that area. Although he did not venture south, the English used Cabot's landing to lay claim to the entire North American continent.

OPPOSITE: Anthony Ashley Cooper, the first Earl of Shaftesbury, was one of the eight proprietors awarded the land of Carolina. Shaftesbury invested much of his personal fortune in the colony.

In 1629, England's King Charles I decided that the time had come to settle the southern coast of America. On October 30th of that year, he granted land, which he called the Province of Carolana, to a nobleman named Robert Heath. The land grant included present-day North and South Carolina and stretched from the Atlantic to the Pacific Ocean. However, Heath was never able to put together an expedition to settle his new land.

For three decades, Carolana lay neglected and forgotten by those in England. Then, in March 1663, King Charles II voided Heath's grant and any claims made by his heirs, and awarded a new charter for the land to eight men who had aided the monarch in the past. Under the new charter, the land was renamed Carolina.

charter—a document that grants a colony the right to exist

The eight men included some of the most important nobles in England. Among them were England's Lord Chancellor, Edward Hyde, Sir William Berkeley, a govenor of the Virginia colony, and Sir John Colleton, a Barbados planter and advocate of slavery in English colonies. However, the most active of the original eight was Anthony Ashley Cooper, the Earl of Shaftesbury. In the coming years, Shaftesbury would help craft the new colony's charter and invest a great deal of his savings to make South Carolina a success.

The eight men were proclaimed the *"true and absolute Lords Proprietors"* of the Carolina

proprietor—a person given ownership and control of a colony

colony. Under the new charter, the proprietors were given the power to control Carolina as they saw fit. They could award land, collect rents and quitrents (taxes on land), and even create a local upper class by granting lord-ships to noble settlers. In turn, the new lords would have the power to rule over the people who lived on their land.

The seal of the Lords Proprietors, created in 1672

Under the charter, the king was to receive a yearly fee from the proprietors and a certain amount of any gold or silver found in the colony. Charles also expected Carolina to serve as a buffer colony between the English colonies to the north and the territory held by England's enemy Spain, to the south. Even after 1670, when England and Spain signed a treaty recognizing the English claim to the Carolinas, the hostility and threat of attack remained.

buffer colony—a colony between two colonies controlled by different countries

For their part, the eight proprietors fully expected the new colony to be a moneymaker for themselves and, later, their heirs. They believed that the warm, temperate climate of the colony would allow settlers to grow grapevines, olive trees, and mulberry trees, which were needed to produce

such valuable trade goods as wine, olive oil, and silk. They
also expected to collect a quitrent, or
yearly fee, from each landowner. In addition,
the proprietors decreed that they would retain ownership
of one-fifth of all the land in Carolina.

quitrent—a tax on land

The proprietors wanted to carefully control how
Carolina developed. *"The land is ours,"* they said, *"and we shall
not part with it but on our own terms."* They believed that
the best way to settle Carolina was to begin by establishing towns in a small area along the coast. This way it
would be easier for the proprietors to control and defend
the colony.

In 1669, before the first settlers set off, Shaftesbury
and his physician, John Locke, wrote up the Fundamental
Constitutions of Carolina, a document meant to lay out the
colony's government and social structure. The constitution
set forth a colony controlled by the upper class. For
example, even though the writers called for a law-making
body called a parliament, made up of both nobles and commoners, only commoners who owned 500 acres (205 ha) of
land could be elected. The Fundamental Constitutions
also contained some democratic ideas, including a provi-
sion for trial by jury and religious toleration. Although the
document was never approved by the Carolina parliament,
the proprietors would do their best to enforce the constitution in the coming years.

PROFILE

John Locke

Today, historians debate whether English philosopher and physician John Locke (1632–1704) or his friend and employer the Earl of Shaftesbury wrote most of the Fundamental Constitutions. However, there is no doubt that Locke authored several other important works. In 1690, he wrote *An Essay Concerning Human Understanding*, which discussed his theories on how people learned. The same year, he wrote *Two Treatises of Government*. In this work, Locke declared that all people had the rights of life, liberty, and land ownership. If a government did not protect these rights, he wrote, then the people had the right to choose a different government. Locke's political theories would influence Thomas Jefferson and other Founders when they drafted the Declaration of Independence and the U.S. Constitution.

Carolina Is for Lovers?

IN A 1666 PAMPHLET, ROBERT HORNE PAINTED CAROLINA as a place where the deserving poor might enjoy a better standard of living. He also described the benefits an Englishwoman might enjoy by migrating to Carolina:

If any maid or single woman have a desire to go over, they will think themselves in the Golden Age, when men paid a dowry for their wives; for if they be but civil, and under 50 years of age, some honest man or other, will purchase them for their wives.

THE FIRST CAROLINA COLONISTS

In August 1669, six years after the Carolina charter was granted, the first colonizing party set sail from England. The three small ships—the *Caroline,* the *Port Royal,* and the *Albemarle*—were under the command of Captain Joseph West and filled with about 90 settlers.

Problems dogged West's group from the start. At stops in Ireland and Barbados, some of the servants who had signed on for the new settlement deserted. The *Port Royal* and the

Albemarle both sank in hurricanes along the way. The *Caroline* finally arrived at what is now Port Royal in March 1670.

After some discussion, a building site was chosen to the north of Port Royal, on a bluff on the west bank of the waterway that the settlers named the Ashley River. The new colonists named the settlement Albemarle Point, but the proprietors would rename it Charles Town. The South Carolina coastal region quickly became known as the lowcountry because of its flat terrain. One observer described the land as *"soe plaine & levyll that it may be compared to a bowling ally."*

bluff—a high cliff

lowcountry—the fertile plantation region along South Carolina's coast and coastal rivers

Another group of early immigrants came from Barbados, an island in the West Indies. An English colony, Barbados was becoming overcrowded with Europeans, and most of the land was owned by just a few wealthy planters. There were few opportunities left for Englishmen to seek their fortune. Some English plantation owners in Barbados believed that Carolina, with its hot summers and fertile soil, would be the perfect place to establish new plantations.

plantation—a large, self-sufficient farm

In 1663, a group of Barbados planters had sent Captain William Hilton to explore the Port Royal area of South Carolina. During his exploration, Captain Hilton named Hilton Head Island for himself. When he returned to Barbados, he brought with him a mostly positive report of the region. *In A Relation of Discovery*, he wrote, *"The natives are* very healthful; we saw many very aged amongst them. The ayr is clear and sweet, the countrey very pleasant and delightful: And we could wish, that all they that want a happy settlement, of our English Nation, were well transported thither."

The Barbadians who came to Carolina brought the colony's first African slaves with them. Some of the Barbadians settled along Goose Creek, a branch of the Cooper River. Here, they helped form a powerful faction known as the Goose Creek Men. They angered the proprietors by trading in Indian slaves, doing business with pirates, and opposing settlers who were not Anglicans, members of the Church of England.

Anglican—a member of the Church of England, a Protestant group

All the early immigrants to Carolina were promised 100 acres (41 ha) each, plus another 100 acres for every servant they brought with them. As a result, many of the settlers brought servants to Carolina. About 240 people who migrated there in the early years were indentured servants. Some indentured servants eventually became very successful in Carolina. In 1700, Edward Hyrne wrote to his brother of one such former servant, "Here is a man in this country that came over a poor servant about 18 to 20 years ago, that has gotten a great estate . . . [and] I am credibly informed that he has now about 4000 head of cattle besides a great number of horses, hogs, etc. and that he had last year 800 calves."

The English colonists were greeted warmly by the Native Americans, who hoped these latest arrivals would protect them from the Spanish. To welcome the English, the Indians *"brought deare skins, some raw, some drest, to trade with us, for which we gave them knives, beads and tobacco and glad they were of the market."* In the coming years, the Indians of the region would help the colonists by trading with them and teaching them fishing and hunting techniques. Later, the Indians would show the settlers the old trading paths into the South Carolina interior.

The earliest map of Carolina was included in the pamphlet "A Brief Description of the Province of Carolina," published in London in 1666. The compass rose shows north as being toward the right margin.

One of the first things the settlers did was to build a stockade for protection against the Spanish and any hostile Indians who might appear. Once that was accomplished, they began working on their own homes within the stockade. Each family received a 10-acre (4-ha) plot of land to garden outside the fortress walls. However, the earliest crops failed, and during the first winter, the settlement's governor, 80-year-old William Sayle, who had arrived in South Carolina with the first immigrants from Barbados, was forced to ration food supplies: *"Noe person . . . shall have or receive . . . any more than five quarts of pease for every man a weeke[,] four quarts . . . for every woman a weeke[,] and three quarts . . . for every child."*

Early letters from Charles Town show that the first colonists were unhappy with the town's officials and the way land was being handed out. The colonists were quick to ask the proprietors for more—more food, more tools, and more money. In 1674, one of the proprietors, Sir Peter Colleton, wrote to Locke, *"Our friends in Carolina sing the same song they did from the beginning, a very healthy, pleasant, and fertile country, but great want of victuals, clothes, and tools."*

It quickly became obvious that the colony was going to take longer to make money than the proprietors had expected. *"Encourage men of estates to remove to Carolina,"* one proprietor wrote to a ship's captain. *"Forbeare to invite the poorer sort yet a while, . . . substantiall men and theire families . . . must make the Plantation which will stock the country with Negroes, Cattle, and other Necessarys, whereas others relye and eate upon us."*

AN INDENTURED SERVANT'S CONTRACT

ONE OF THE FIRST COLONISTS IN SOUTH CAROLINA WAS Samuell Morris, who came as the indentured servant of Captain Joseph West. The full term of Morris's indenture was two years and three weeks. During that time, he was required to work aboard one of West's ships or on land, as his master commanded. However, West had obligations, too:

And in consideration whereof the said Joseph West doth promise to allow ye said Sam Morris sufficient meat and drinke and at ye end of one year & three weeks to pay the said Sam Morris five pound or the value of it in goods att Barbados, or Virginia, or Carolina, as Sam Morris shall desire it and at the expiration of the other year to pay him five pounds more.

Despite the rumblings of discontent, Charles Town slowly grew. In February 1671, a second group of 64 colonists arrived from England, followed by even more white Europeans from Barbados. In 1672, nearly 100 settlers came from New York to the new colony, attracted by the proprietors' offers of land. By the mid-1670s, about 400 settlers made their homes in Carolina.

CHAPTER THREE

Life Under the Proprietors

CHARLES TOWN BECOMES A THRIVING PORT CITY, *but the outskirts of the colony remain dangerous and difficult to inhabit. Carolina has trouble attracting more settlers.*

B y 1680, about 1,000 settlers had made their home in the colony of Carolina. But, after a decade of slow growth, officials decided to move the small settlement across the river to Oyster Point, a peninsula where the Ashley and Cooper Rivers meet. The new location was easier to defend, and its deep natural harbor would be perfect for trade and transportation. The new town kept its name—Charles Town—and the colony's first permanent settlement was born.

OPPOSITE: This image of the fort at Charles Town, built between the Ashley and Cooper Rivers, shows Native Americans and English settlers conducting trade in the busy harbor town.

The new town was carefully planned. Following what was called the "Grand Modell of Charles Town," the streets were laid out in a grid, with a large square at the intersection of the main streets. Government buildings would soon rise in the square, making it the center of the colony's government. The entire town was surrounded by a wall to keep the colonists safe from Spanish and Indian attacks.

Carolina was run by a governor, a council, and an assembly. The governor and half the council members were handpicked by the proprietors. The job of the council was to propose laws for the colony. The assembly was elected by the colonists (representatives had to own 500 acres of land as set forth in the Fundamental Constitutions) but this body had very little real power. Although the assembly weighed in on matters with a vote, any laws enacted or decisions made had to be approved by the proprietors. At this time, Carolina was divided into three large counties located along the coast: Craven, Berkeley, and Colleton.

A Growing Town

THOMAS NEWE, A UNIVERSITY-educated Englishman who traveled to South Carolina in 1682, sent a letter to his father to describe the new settlement of Charles Town: *The town which two years since had but 3 or 4 houses, hath now about a hundred houses in it, all which are wholy built of wood....*

Through the governor, the proprietors pressured the assembly to ratify the Fundamental Constitutions. When the colonists refused, the proprietors warned that few people would want to settle in a land with no written constitution: *"Nor will people come there until things are better settled, nor can wee with honour or a good conscience invite men to come amongst you."* The proprietors also warned of more dire consequences: *"Your numbers will by degree be soe diminished that you will be easily cut off by the Indians or pyrates."*

FAR FROM PARADISE

South Carolina had a reputation as a dangerous and unhealthy place. Although the land was fertile, the hot, humid Carolina summers surprised English settlers. In their woolen clothing, the colonists found that even the smallest tasks made them sweaty and exhausted. The settlers from Barbados, who expected a tropical climate, were surprised by the winter freezes, frosts, and snowfall that killed plants and crops. Hurricanes, lightning storms, and the occasional tornado also caused damage in the colony.

There were also natural dangers lurking in the Carolina wilds. Poisonous snakes could be found throughout the colony. Some even found their way into the settlers' homes. Alligators lazed in Carolina's rivers and swamps. The forests were home to panthers, wildcats, and bears that would attack and eat calves and sheep.

An alligator suns itself on a log in a cypress swamp in South Carolina. Dangerous wildlife and diseases carried by insects were a problem for early settlers in the colony.

Epidemics of disease were also a serious problem in Carolina. Each year, outbreaks of disease killed many colonists. During two months in 1699, for example, about 160 residents of Charles Town died as the result of a yellow fever epidemic, described as *"a most infectious, pestilential & mortall distemper [fatal illness]."* Children and newly arrived settlers were at the highest risk, but the colony's chief justice and about half the assembly members also died.

epidemic—the rapid spread of disease to a large population of people

yellow fever—an infectious disease caused by the bite of a mosquito

A ROUGH START

JUDITH GITON MANIGAULT WAS 20 YEARS OLD WHEN SHE came to Charles Town in 1685. Like other Huguenots, Manigault had fled from France, traveling first to Holland, then Germany, then finally to England in search of religious freedom and economic opportunity. After arriving in South Carolina, she wrote a letter to her brother describing conditions in the colony:

After our arrival in Carolina, we suffered every kind of evil. In about eighteen months our elder brother, unaccustomed to the hard labor we had to undergo, died of a fever. Since leaving France we had experienced every kind of affliction—disease—famine—pestilence—poverty—hard labor. I have been for six months together without tasting bread, working the ground like a slave.

ATTRACTING NEW SETTLERS

To attract more immigrants to Carolina, the proprietors advertised in England, Scotland, the Netherlands, and other countries. They targeted groups seeking to escape religious persecution. The proprietors avoided talking about the negative aspects of settling in Carolina, highlighting instead the colony's well-known religious toleration and the wealth of available land there. Groups of French Huguenots, Scottish Protestants, and many others were willing to face the dangers in a new land in order to enjoy the freedom to practice their religions. As a result, Carolina became one of the most diverse colonies in America.

Groups of French Huguenots began arriving in Carolina around 1680. Their numbers increased in 1685, when Louis XIV of France revoked a law that had allowed Protestants in the country to legally practice their religion. As a result, many Huguenots fled the country. About 500 settled in Carolina—most along the Santee River in Craven County.

Among the Huguenots who migrated were black-smiths, carpenters, silversmiths, shipbuilders, and weavers. They quickly established their own businesses in the colony and many became quite successful.

In 1684, a small group of Protestants from Scotland migrated to Carolina. The proprietors agreed to allow the Covenanters, as they were known, to establish their own government within the colony at Port Royal. In 1686, the new settlement was destroyed and most of the colonists killed when a force of Spaniards and Indians attacked and burned the small town.

Groups of Jews began arriving in Carolina in the early 1700s. Most were Sephardic Jews, Jewish people from Portugal and Spain, persecuted there and

Sephardic Jew—a person from Portugal or Spain whose religious faith is Judaism

fleeing for their lives. Later, many Jews from Germany also migrated to Carolina. Charles Town became home to the largest Jewish population in the American colonies.

Workers hoe the soil, tending crops while another stands guard against wild animals.

EKING OUT A LIVING

The early colonial economy depended upon trade with Indians of the area. Westo, Cubaso, and Creek traded deerskins to the colonists in exchange for guns, ammunition, alcohol, and other items. The traders would then bring the skins into Charles Town and sell them to merchants there. The merchants, in turn, would ship the hides to merchants in Europe, where deerskin was in high demand for clothing.

Henry Woodward

In 1666, a young doctor named Henry Woodward (1646–1686) chose to live in the Carolina wilderness to learn the languages of the native peoples. In the coming years, Woodward's knowledge would serve him well, allowing him to establish trade relations with many tribes in the area. In 1685, Woodward traveled into present-day Georgia and convinced the Creek to trade with Carolina's settlers. As a result of this trip, Carolina took over the trade in deerskins that had been controlled by the Spanish and the Virginia colony. Woodward also went on various peace-making missions, helping to maintain good relations between the natives and the colonists. Woodward's travels throughout the southern colonies helped mapmakers create more accurate maps of the region.

Some of the first problems between the colonists and proprietors arose when the proprietors tried to take control of the trade with the Indians. They also wanted to put an end to the enslavement of Indians in the region. The proprietors worked through agents like Henry Woodward to monopolize the trade in deerskins and removed men from office who took part in the native slave trade. In response, the traders, many of them Goose Creek Men, stirred up a war with Woodward's Indian allies, the Westos, in 1680. By 1681, Carolina colonists had wiped out most of the Westo tribe, selling any survivors into slavery. The Goose Creek Men were now firmly in control of the Indian trade.

Carolina had few goods that other Colonies wanted. Instead, the Carolina colonists traded with England, the West Indies, and privateers. During the late 1600s, pirates roamed the Atlantic coast and the Caribbean, preying on French and Spanish ships. With their ships filled with stolen goods, the pirates would sail to Carolina to exchange their booty for food. This illegal trade continued into the early 1700s.

privateer—a privately owned ship or its captain hired by a government to attack and rob the ships of enemy countries

Another important industry during early colonial days was the trade in naval supplies, including timber, tar, and pitch. Shipbuilders used Carolina's tall pine trees to make strong ships' masts. Most of the wood products were sent to the West Indies, as were extra food crops, deerskins, and salted beef and pork.

Around 1685, the first rice crops were planted in Carolina. The swampy, fertile soil around the lowcountry rivers and creeks was perfect for rice fields, which needed to be flooded periodically with fresh water. By 1700, the colony's rice crop showed signs of its future importance. That year, rice planters shipped 300 tons (272 metric tons) to England and 30 tons (27 metric tons) to the West Indies.

The success of the rice crop in Carolina caused plantation owners to move farther inland to escape possible
flooding by the ocean. It also greatly increased the demand
for workers in the colony. Because it was believed that
European workers were unsuited for hard labor in the hot
Carolina sun, plantation owners looked elsewhere. They
bought Indian and African slaves in ever-increasing numbers
to cultivate their land.

THE SEEDS OF A
SERIOUS PROBLEM

The late 1600s and early 1700s were times of turmoil in
Carolina. In 1690, Governor James Colleton, chosen by the
proprietors, was ousted from office by the colonial
assembly. Two years later, assembly members sent a list of
14 grievances to the proprietors in London.

The colonists' main complaint was the unfair way the
proprietors awarded land. They believed the proprietors
parceled out the best land for themselves and their friends.

In 1695, proprietor John Archdale arrived in Carolina to
serve as governor and to work out the problems between the
proprietors and the colonists. In one year's time, Archdale
standardized the price for land in the colony. He also
reformed the quitrent system, forgiving past-due quitrents in
some cases and allowing new settlers to abstain from paying
quitrents for their first five years in the colony. ✹

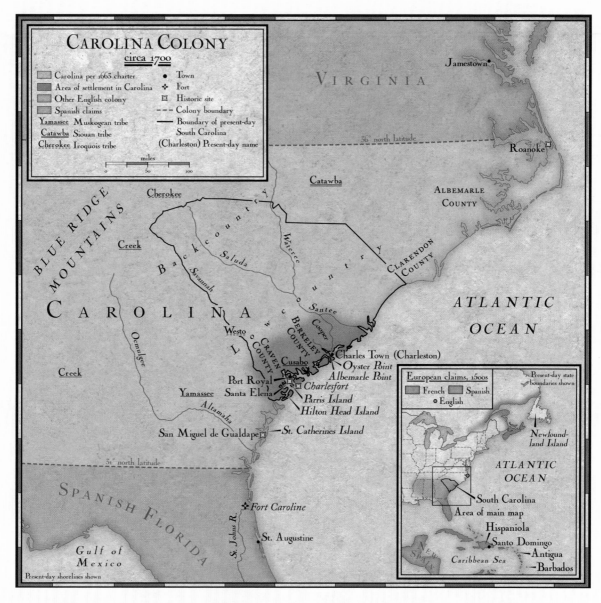

This map shows the area of Carolina Colony in 1700 and the Indian tribes who were native to the region. Although the Spanish, the French, and English had explored the region and attempted settlements in the 1500s (see inset map), it was the English who succeeded in establishing a permanent presence in 1670. Settlement was along the coast, with Charles Town the center of trade and government.

CHAPTER FOUR

A Rocky Time

THE EARLY 1700S BRING ARMED CONFLICT *to Carolina,*
until the English finally eliminate all threat of French and
Spanish takeovers. Politics and religion divide settlers.
The colony officially splits into two, North and South
Carolina, on the eve of war with the Yamassee.

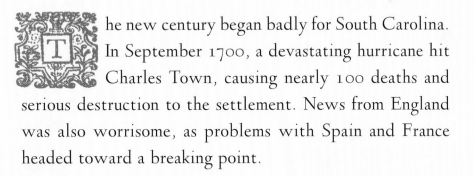

T he new century began badly for South Carolina.
In September 1700, a devastating hurricane hit
Charles Town, causing nearly 100 deaths and
serious destruction to the settlement. News from England
was also worrisome, as problems with Spain and France
headed toward a breaking point.

OPPOSITE: Governor Charles Craven of South Carolina leads colonists
into battle against the Yamassee at the Combahee River in the
southern lowcountry in 1715.

In 1702, England and its allies—Austria, the Netherlands, and parts of the Holy Roman Empire—declared war on Spain and France. The war spilled over to the colonies in North America, where the

conflict became known as Queen Anne's War. The war dragged on until 1713, leaving Carolina colonists in a constant state of fear. Both the Spanish and the French were within striking distance of South Carolina: Spain in St. Augustine and the French in Mobile, Alabama, founded in 1702. In addition, colonists worried about attacks by the Indian allies of the French.

Soon after the war began, Carolina officials decided to mount an attack against St. Augustine. James Moore, the governor of Carolina from 1700 to 1703, hoped to defeat the Spanish and then continue through Florida to the Gulf of Mexico and wipe out Mobile. In November 1702, Moore led 500 colonists and 300 native allies to the outskirts of St. Augustine. They laid siege to the settlement's strong fortress, where the town residents had fled for protection. After two months, reinforcements from Spain arrived to help the Spanish residents, and Moore's army was forced to retreat. Before they left, they burned churches and other buildings outside the fortress walls. Moore would launch attacks on the Spanish in Florida in 1704 and again in 1706. Forces wiped out most of the mission settlements in the Spanish colony.

THE FIRST CAROLINA CURRENCY

AFTER GOVERNOR MOORE'S 1702 attack on St. Augustine, Carolina found itself in debt. In addition to purchasing guns and ammunition, colonial officials had spent money to strengthen Charles Town's defenses. In all, the colony was in debt about £4,000 sterling (about $960,000 in today's dollars).

To ease the money shortage, the Carolina government issued the colony's first paper money. The new currency, called "Country bills," was printed in denominations ranging from £20 ($4,800) to 50 shillings ($600). The interest-earning bills were purchased by colonists with rice and other goods. They could use the bills to pay taxes other than quitrents.

In 1706, French and Spanish troops mounted their last major effort to wipe out England's southernmost colony in what is now the United States. (Georgia had not yet been founded.) In August, five French ships plus Spanish troops from St. Augustine gathered around Charles Town. The colonists drove off the invaders, and by the end of the month the colony was once again safe.

INTERNAL PROBLEMS

The early 1700s were also a period of inner turmoil in Carolina. Carolinians were increasingly unhappy with the way the absent proprietors were governing the colony. One of the major points of contention was the manner in which the proprietors awarded land. In addition, they were now putting pressure on colonists to pay their quitrents. While new

An unruly crowd of Charleston colonists expresses its displeasure with the political system during an election in 1701.

colonists had been granted a five-year grace period in 1695, earlier colonists had chosen not to pay at all.

In 1702, the proprietors instructed their quitrent collector in Carolina to begin suing those who had not paid. When this attempt failed to work effectively, the proprietors halted all large land sales and gifts except ones that they personally agreed on. Rumors now flew that the proprietors were planning to repossess the land of any colonist who owed them quitrents. Although the proprietors had no such plan, the colonial council quickly passed a law that made such repossessions illegal.

Another serious source of strife in the colony was the question of religion. When Carolina was first founded, the proprietors had encouraged people of many religions to settle there. By the early 1700s, about half of all the colonists in Carolina were members of the Church of England, the official religion of England and the religion of the proprietors. The other half, most of them

Dissenter—a Protestant in South Carolina who did not belong to the Church of England

from various Protestant sects, were known as Dissenters. Dissenters, although still members of the Church of England, wanted to worship differently than the local churches dictated.

In 1704, the assembly, led by Anglican governor Robert Johnson, passed the Church Act, banning all Dissenters from serving in future assemblies. Chief Justice Nicholas Trott later gave his reason for passing the law: *"They [the Dissenters] never did any good there nor never will do any."*

In 1706, the Church Act was amended. The new law made the Church of England the official church of the colony. Dissenters and colonists of other religions had to pay a tax to support the church and pay the salaries of Anglican ministers. However, the new law allowed Dissenters to serve in the assembly and practice their religion and build churches of their own. At this time, many Huguenots became Anglicans in order to avoid paying the church tax. The new law also divided the colony into ten parishes, which became the major units of government in Carolina.

parish—a district in colonial South Carolina that served as the unit of local government

Resentment against the French Huguenots and other Dissenters continued in the colony. For example, Carolina officials attempted to bar Huguenots from owning ships because they were not English citizens. This issue was resolved in 1708, when the British Parliament passed a law that made all Huguenots in British lands citizens.

Parliament— Great Britain's law-making body

By 1709, about 9,580 people lived in what is now South Carolina. In 1712, the proprietors separated Carolina into two sections, South Carolina and North Carolina. The split allowed proprietors to focus on developing the more profitable South Carolina. Although now a separate colony, North Carolina was still governed by a deputy sent from Charles Town to the south. This arrangement continued until 1729, when they both became a royal colonies.

The problems in South Carolina during the early 1700s earned the colony a reputation as a place that was in constant turmoil and uproar. Historians believe that it undoubtedly deterred many people from coming to Carolina.

THE YAMASSEE WAR

In 1715, colonists in South Carolina faced a danger that would prove even more serious than the threat of attack by the French and Spanish. That year, the Yamassee, Catawba, Creek, and a dozen other tribes rose up in anger against the colonists in the Yamassee War (1715–1717).

Problems among these tribes and the colonists stretched back to the earliest days of trading between them. Over the past decades, the Yamassee and other tribes had suffered at the hands of unscrupulous Carolina traders, the Goose Creek Men. The traders were rugged men who moved into the Carolina interior to live in the woods, near the Indians.

As the traders pushed farther into the Carolina frontier, they caused turmoil. Some stirred up Indian wars in order to enslave the losing tribe members. After 1690, thousands of Indians were sold as slaves in Charles Town. The traders also brought alcohol and disease with them.

The proprietors and Carolina officials knew that it was in the best interests of the colony to maintain good relations with the native tribes of the region. In 1707, Carolina lawmakers passed laws to regulate the traders. The laws required traders to buy a license and banned them from trading rum to the Indians. The law also appointed Indian agents, men who traveled into the interior and lived with the tribes. The agents had authority to free wrongly enslaved Indians and punish traders who beat or abused the natives. However, traders refused to follow the new laws, and the Indian agents proved powerless to enforce them. As more colonists moved into the interior in search of plantation land, the Indians became even angrier at the loss of their lands.

A Yamassee warrior, carrying a bloody stick, readies his tribe for battle in this 1715 painting called "Signal from Yamassee Uprising in South Carolina."

In April 1715, the natives attacked some of the European settlements in South Carolina. Many settlers were killed. One of the first victims of the Yamassee War was the Indian agent, Thomas Nairne. When the war erupted, Nairne was visiting the Yamassee tribe in an effort to keep the peace. Although he had been a friend of the Indians, he now became a symbol of the hated colonists. Nairne was tortured and killed. In 1716, as many as 700 Indians came within a few miles of Charles Town before they were scared off by the Carolina militia. The war dragged on for two years, with the natives launching guerrilla attacks throughout the colony. About 400 colonists died during the war, and many more were driven north from their settlements to the shelter of Charles Town or towns in North Carolina and Virginia. The war also caused great economic damage to the colony. Buildings were burned, crops were destroyed, and livestock were driven away. The war finally ended after the Yamassee, their numbers dwindling, were driven out of the colony and into their original homelands in Northern Florida. In South Carolina, remaining Indians such as the Creek were forced to accept a peace treaty with the colonists.

militia—a group of citizen-soldiers organized to defend a colony

guerrilla—describing a type of combat in which small groups of fighters carry out surprise attacks against an enemy

The conflict marked an end to the trade in Indian slaves in the region and ended any power Native

Americans may have had left in South Carolina. It also worsened the problems between the colonists and the proprietors. During the war, Carolina had appealed to the proprietors for troops and military supplies, but they received very little aid. Other Colonies had refused the pleas for aid, too.

PUTTING AN END TO PIRACY

In the early 1700s, Carolina officials also had to address the problem of piracy. During Queen Anne's War, privateers had attacked and robbed Spanish and French ships. Now, with the war over, they threatened British and colonial ships.

By the late 1600s, South Carolina was exporting and importing a wide variety of goods. The colony had trade relations with England, the West Indies, and several colonies to the north. Charles Town merchants no longer needed to trade with the outlaws.

One of the area's most notorious pirates was Edward Teach, better known as Blackbeard. Blackbeard, who used the uninhabited islands along the coast of North Carolina as his home base, began raiding colonial and Caribbean settlements after 1713. He reportedly struck terror into the hearts of his victims by placing slow-burning pieces of rope in his hair and his long black beard and lighting them on fire. In May 1718, Blackbeard and 300 pirates sailed into Charles Town harbor. The pirate held some of the town's citizens for ransom and threatened to burn down the port city unless he was given medicine for his crew. True to his word, he left after his demands were met.

South Carolina colonists now demanded government action to bring the pirates to justice. In the summer of 1718, Virginia's governor sent British ships out to catch the outlaws—dead or alive. In September, Stede Bonnet, the "gentleman pirate," was caught and put to death at Charles Town with 29 members of his crew. In November, another pirate captain named Richard Worley was captured and hanged at Charles Town, along with 19 of his men. Blackbeard himself was killed days later while battling the British Navy off the coast of North Carolina.

"The Buccaneers" by Frederick Judd Waugh, illustrates a heated battle between British soldiers and pirates who are tyring to take over their ship.

DEFYING THE PROPRIETORS

In 1718, the South Carolina assembly sent several laws to Britain for approval by the proprietors. Despite their insistence on overseeing the assembly, the proprietors usually signed off on all the laws sent to them. But, this time was different. The proprietors wanted to take firmer control of the colony. When they received this new set of laws, they decided to send a message by vetoing them. They also halted all land grants.

In 1719, when the colonists learned of the proprietors' vetoes, they were furious. Assembly members decided to ignore any vetoes from the proprietors. They also asked the present governor, Robert Johnson, to *"hold the reins of government for the King till his Majesty's pleasure be known."* Although Johnson had been appointed by the proprietors, he was respected for his competence. The control of the government was now firmly in the hands of the assembly and the council.

Although they now had no control over the South Carolina government, the proprietors refused to give up their rights to the land immediately. The proprietors in London would continue causing problems for ten years, but their rule was over. From 1719 until 1729, the Board of Trade, which had been formed in 1696 by King William III to oversee England's commercial interests in all its colonies, managed South Carolina'a growth and welfare. ▨

Board of Trade—a committee formed in 1696 to oversee England's commercial interests in its colonies

CHAPTER FIVE

South Carolina Prospers

SOUTH CAROLINA PROSPERS *as the demand for rice and indigo increases throughout Europe and the Colonies. A class system emerges as a result of plantation life, effecting politics and growth.*

I n 1721, Sir Francis Nicholson, the provisional governor appointed by the king, arrived in South Carolina. Nicholson's task was to make peace and mend relations between the fighting factions within the colony. He hoped to ease the conflicts between Anglicans and Dissenters, merchants and planters, and supporters and opponents of the proprietors. Unfortunately, Nicholson accomplished little, and he was recalled in 1725.

OPPOSITE: Drayton Hall, a plantation house near Charles Town, was built in 1742 along the Ashley River. It still stands today in near-original condition and can be visited by the public.

South Carolina remained without a governor until 1729. During that time, the economy continued to suffer. With the colony's status up in the air, settlers received no help from either the Board of Trade or the proprietors.

Finally, in 1729, the Board of Trade and the proprietors reached an agreement about the colony. The proprietors agreed to sell their interest in South Carolina for £2,500 (about $530,000 today) each, plus a £5,000 (about $1 million today) lump sum payment on all quitrents owed to them. South Carolina became a royal colony.

The Board of Trade chose former governor Robert Johnson to be the colony's first royal governor. Johnson, who governed South Carolina from 1729 to 1735, encouraged new arrivals to settle in the interior section of the colony known as the backcountry. The governor also made it easier for the wealthy to purchase large chunks of land there.

backcountry—South Carolina's rugged interior

During Johnson's tenure, the colony of Georgia was founded to the south. The new colony, now the southernmost of Britain's 13 American colonies, would become the new buffer against the Spanish in Florida.

NEW SETTLERS AND ECONOMIC PROSPERITY

In 1720, nearly 19,000 people—7,000 whites and 11,800 black slaves—lived in South Carolina. Throughout the decade, that number grew steadily. In 1726, a small group of Swiss Huguenots arrived. The following year, a number of Irish Protestants joined 500 others already living in the southern section of the colony. Later, Germans arrived to help settle the interior, as did groups of Welsh Baptists from Delaware and Pennsylvania.

Under Governor Johnson's control, the pace of settlement in the colony increased. New immigrants to South Carolina were offered 50 acres (20 ha) each, plus their transportation costs and some farm equipment to get them started. By 1732, six new townships had been founded in the backcountry.

Robert Johnson, Governor of the South Carolina colony, was popular with most residents for spurring settlement and fighting pirates. This illustration shows him being hailed as a hero after returning home.

Between 1720 and 1730, it is believed that the black population in the colony doubled. As the colony's economy became dependent upon rice, more and more slaves were imported to work the fields. Merchants, traders, shop-keepers, and skilled craftsmen all bought large parcels of land and started rice plantations. By 1775, the colony would export more than 70 million pounds (31.8 million kg) of rice each year.

Another important Carolina cash crop got its start in 1739. That year, 16-year-old Eliza Lucas began experi-menting with indigo plants on her father's South Carolina plantations. Indigo is used to make a deep blue dye. In the coming years, indigo would become the second most impor-tant crop in the colony.

This illustration shows how indigo is prepared for market. Slaves carry bushels of the harvested plant to a series of water-filled tubs (foreground). After many hours of soaking, the foul-smelling rotting indigo is stirred and beaten with paddles. After the water is drained off, the remaining pudding-like mixture is scooped into molds for drying. When completely hardened, the blue dye is cut into squares for sale.

Eliza Lucas Pinckney

Eliza Lucas (1722–1793) and her family migrated from Antigua, a British colony in the West Indies, to South Carolina in 1738. Colonel Lucas purchased three plantations, including Wappoo, located about 17 miles (27 km) from Charles Town. Soon after the family arrived, however, Colonel Lucas was called back to military service in the West Indies.

Eliza, only 16 years old, was now left to care for her sickly mother and her younger sister—all while managing her father's plantations. She wrote a friend in 1740,

I have the business of 3 plantations to transact, which requires much writing and more business and fatigue of other sorts than you can imagine. But least you should imagine it too burthensome to a girl at my early time of life, give me leave to answer you: I think myself happy that I can be useful to so good a father, and by rising very early I find I can go through much business.

When she was 21, Eliza married Charles Pinckney, a wealthy plantation owner and politician. Two of their sons would play important roles in the fight for independence from Britain. When Eliza Pinckney died in 1793, George Washington asked to help carry her coffin to the cemetery.

PLANTATION ELITE

By the mid-1730s, it was clear that the plantation system would be the mainstay of South Carolina's colonial economy. As their wealth grew, plantation owners became the colony's elite, dominating South Carolina economically, socially, and politically.

The newly wealthy plantation owners worked hard to create an upper-class society, modeled on England's aristocracy. They patterned their plantation homes and Charles Town townhouses on the mansions and estates in England. They even named their plantations for landmarks in England, such as Kensington, Hyde Park, and Hampton. They planted magnificent gardens filled with flowers, shrubs, and trees imported from England.

Fine furniture, curtains, and rugs for the Carolina mansions were imported directly from England. Plantation owners sat down to dinner with china and silverware sent from England. Expensive wines and other delicacies were imported from Europe. The planters, along with their wives and children, wore only the latest fashions, sent from Europe on the latest ship.

With overseers and slaves doing most of the work on the plantations, the Carolina upper class had plenty of time to enjoy leisure activities. In addition to hunting and fishing, the wealthy enjoyed dice playing and cards. Gambling on horse races and cockfights was a popular pastime.

THE MARK OF A GENTLEMAN

DURING COLONIAL TIMES, GENTLEMAN PLANTERS HAD SERVANTS with them at all times. A visitor to the colony commented:

A gentn. On horseback hove in sight who appeared by his dress, his air & the goodness of his horse to be of some note & distinction. . . . One of the company finished . . . by saying "he cannot be a gentleman for his is riding without servants." So it is that in this country a person can no more act or move without an attending servant than a planet without its sattellites. If they only cross their plantation they must have a subservient follower.

The plantation owner's wife was responsible for the management of the household servants. Women had free time, too, which they spent visiting other plantation ladies, reading, or embroidering. One of their most important roles was organizing dinner parties and dances for other members of Carolina's elite.

Plantation society dominated Charles Town. Because plantations were often located far from each other, the Carolina capital served as the meeting place and playground for the wealthy. Plantation families usually spent the social season after the harvest in their city townhouses.

Unlike the English aristocracy, South Carolina's wealthy planters were not concerned about how people made their money. The planters, however, were very conscious of being the colony's elite class. They looked down upon backcountry settlers and those of lesser means and believed that they were entitled to control the government in the colony. Soon, this attitude would cause serious problems for South Carolina.

Southern Hospitality

PLANTATION OWNERS WERE HAPPY to receive visitors and loved to show off their wealth. In 1734, a visitor from England wrote, *"The Gentlemen in general, in this country, are exceeding civil to strangers, so that a man, if he knows but the nature of the country, may go from one plantation to another, for a year or two . . . and the gentlemen will be always glad of his company."* Not everyone was so impressed. A colonist who migrated from England wrote home, *"The Greatest Misfortune that attends it [Charles Town] is the Hypocrisie and Knavery of its Inhabitants for they are to the Last Degree Ignorant and Opini[on]ated. . . . They are trained up in Luxury and are the Greatest Debauchees in Nature."*

THRIVING CHARLES TOWN

By the 1760s, only one out of every four white colonists lived in the lowcountry. However, this small group controlled 86 percent of all taxable wealth in the colony and owned 90 percent of all slaves.

Charles Town became a thriving cultural center. Wealthy or well-connected visitors to the city could attend balls, concerts, or plays performed at the Dock Street Theater, built in 1736. The theater, one of the finest of its time, was described as *"elegantly finished and supposed for the size to be the most commodius [spacious] on the continent."*

The avenue in front of the customs house was one of the main streets in Charles Town. A large palmetto stands in the town square.

Many planters were members of one or more of the various social clubs in Charles Town. One of the first was the St. Andrew's Society, founded in 1729. This charitable organization, originally founded by the colony's Scottish population, held an annual parade on November 30th, St. Andrew's Day. Other clubs were founded for those

America's First
FEMALE PUBLISHER

In 1738, Elizabeth Timothy's husband, Lewis, died from an *"unhappy Accident."* Lewis had taken over as publisher of the *South Carolina Gazette* soon after its founder, Thomas Whitmarsh died. Already a mother of six, a pregnant Elizabeth would soon have seven children to support. So she took control of her husband's printing press and continued to publish the paper. Shortly after beginning, she placed the following announcement in the colonial paper: *"I take this Opportunity of informing the Publick, that I shall continue the said Paper as usual; and hope, by the Assistance of my Friends, to make it as entertaining and correct as may be reasonably expected."*

Elizabeth Timothy, born in Holland, had migrated to South Carolina with her French Huguenot husband in 1731. With Lewis gone, she published the paper under the name of her eldest son, 13-year-old Peter. As official printer for the colony, she also printed bills and laws for the government. Elizabeth probably served as the paper's publisher and editor until 1746, when her son Peter turned 21. After he took over the business, she opened a small book and stationery shop next door.

Later, Benjamin Franklin paid her the highest of compliments: *"[She] managed the business with such success, that she not only brought up reputably a family of children, but, at the expiration of the term, was able to purchase of me the printing house, and establish her son in it."*

who enjoyed literary discussions, hunting, and pastimes. Later, before the Revolution, patriotic societies would spring up in Charles Town.

Charles Town was also home to a thriving middle class, made up of carpenters, silversmiths, teachers, shopkeepers, and many others. By the early 1730s, South Carolina had its own printer, located in Charles Town. On January 8, 1732, the first issue of the *South Carolina Gazette* went on sale. The paper was founded by Benjamin Franklin and Thomas Whitmarsh, an English printer who moved from Philadelphia to Charles Town around 1731. The *Gazette* would continue publication for more than four decades.

Less well-to-do people living outside Charles Town flocked to the city to witness slave auctions, executions, and the fireworks and bonfires that took place during the celebration of the king's birthday each year. They could also enjoy a mug of ale at a local inn or tavern.

Despite the city's reputation as the most sophisticated colonial center of its time, Charles Town had an unpleasant side. As in other colonial cities, garbage was thrown into the streets to be eaten by roaming pigs. Pickpockets and other criminals plied their trades after dark. Groups of slaves would meet at street corners after dark to play dice and drink. One wealthy citizen complained of the "*unmannerly, rude, and insolent slaves . . . profanely swearing, cursing, and talking obscenely.*" As a result, the elite citizens began using carriages to get about town. ❄

CHAPTER SIX

Slavery in Carolina

AFRICAN SLAVES ENDURE horrible conditions working the colony's plantations. Slave laws are passed to prevent rebellion and loss.

he first African slaves were brought into South Carolina in the early 1670s by migrants from Barbados. Slavery was well established in Barbados, an English colony since 1627. As the trade in Native American slaves dwindled after 1715, planters brought African slaves into the South Carolina in ever-increasing numbers. Charles Town, one of the largest ports in the colonies, became a major slaving port. Between 1706 and 1775, about 93,000 slaves were brought into South

OPPOSITE: Slave traders on horseback herd a group of Africans along a river, heading to a slave market in the south. Traders who were unable to sell all their slaves in one market would travel to other areas hoping to sell their property elsewhere.

Carolina, primarily from Africa and the Caribbean. Most of the enslaved people brought into Carolina remained in the colony to work on rice, indigo, and other plantations.

These imported slaves were brought first to the pesthouse on Sullivan's Island in Charles Town's harbor. Here, men, women, and children were quarantined for at least ten days. They were bathed and observed for signs of smallpox, dysentery, and other contagious diseases.

pesthouse—a place where slaves were screened for disease and isolated to prevent them from infecting healthy people

Slaves who were sick were kept on the island until they got better or died. Today, Sullivan's Island is known as the "Ellis Island of black America."

Slave sales were usually held at the town wharves, merchants' stores, or at "fairs" where the slaves were sold alongside other goods. Newspapers and broadsides (printed announcements) spread the word when a cargo of slaves arrived in Charles Town. Strong young black men between the ages of 14 and 25 were sold for the highest prices. Black women from 14 to 20 also brought good prices. One slave trader advised, *"Let your*

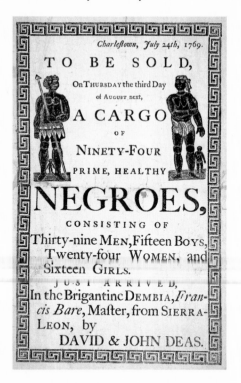

This flier advertises a new shipment of slaves from Africa, announcing the time and location of their sale by David and John Deas.

purchase be of the very best kind of slaves, black & smooth, free from blemishes, Young & well grown, the more Men the better, but not old." By 1770, a good slave might sell for 40 pounds sterling (about $7,000 today). Slaves from West Africa were especially prized by Carolina planters because they knew how to grow rice and indigo.

LIFE ON A RICE PLANTATION

Most of the slaves in South Carolina were sent to work on rice plantations. Life on the rice plantations was very difficult for slaves. They were kept busy year-round, performing the dirty, backbreaking work of planting, cultivating, reaping, and preparing the grain for market. In the years ahead, slaves in colonies to the north would dread being "sold south" to work in South Carolina and Georgia.

To prepare a field for planting, slaves first had to remove cypress and other trees in the swampy areas. Next, they built the ditches and dams used to channel freshwater into the rice fields. Floodgates were constructed to allow water to flow into and out of the fields, as needed. The slaves working in the swampy fields had to brave poisonous snakes and disease-carrying insects. As many as one out of every three lowcountry slaves died within the first year of their arrival.

One European visitor to South Carolina recorded his observations on rice planting:

If a work could be imagined peculiarly unwholesome, and even
fatal to health, it must be that of standing like the Negross
[Negroes] ancle and even mid-leg deep in water, which floats on
ouzy mud; and exposed all the while to a burning sun, which
makes the very air they breathe hotter than the human blood
. . . a more horrible employment can hardly be imagined.

In March or April, slaves began sowing the rice in the rectangular fields. As the tall rice grass began to grow, slaves tended it, weeding, flooding, and hoeing the fields. "Bird minders" scared away bobolinks, "rice birds" that flocked to the paddies in the late summer to eat the ripening rice. Then, in September, the slaves began harvesting the rice, gathering the cut grass into bundles to be processed.

Processing rice was an exacting and time-consuming task that included removing the edible grain from its outer husk, then preparing the rice for storing and shipping. Slaves processed the rice by hand, using a technique probably brought from West Africa. To remove the husk, the rice was milled, or ground, with a wooden mortar and pestle between 3 and 5 feet (1 and 1.5 m) long. Slaves had to put just the right amount of pressure on the husks when grinding.

After the milling, the rice and empty husks were placed into a flat basket for winnowing. During winnowing, slaves shook the baskets so that the husks moved to the edge and could be removed and thrown away. Once again, the rice was pounded, this time to remove the grain's hard brown outer shell.

Slaves winnow rice in a special basket, cleaning the dirt and loose husks from the dried plants. The woman in the middle hulls, or mills, the rice by pounding it with a tool that removes any remaining husks.

Planters pushed the slaves to complete the time-consuming process by early winter, so the rice could be shipped to Europe by February, when prices were at their highest. Until the time came to plant another crop, slaves had plenty of other tasks to perform—processing indigo, tending seasonal crops, and repairing the fields, ditches, and fences of the plantation.

Slaves in South Carolina worked under the task system. When the slaves finished their tasks for the day, they were allowed to tend to their own gardens and families.

However, with so much to be accomplished on the plantation, slaves were often kept busy from sunup to sundown.

Not all plantation slaves were field hands. There were also house servants who cooked, cleaned, and cared for the master's children. Other slaves were spared field duty because of their skills at carpentry, blacksmithing, or other crafts. Skilled slaves were especially valuable because they could be hired out to other planters.

This oil painting shows a one-room slave shack surrounded by a dirt yard with little shade, a few chickens, and dinner cooking over an open fire. Such primitive structures were found on many southern plantations.

Human Property

Plantation owners were not concerned about their slaves' quality of life. They housed their "property" in small, rickety cabins with little or no furniture. Some slaves did not even have a bed to rest in after a long day's work, sleeping instead on the dirt floor, covered by a blanket. For food, the slaves were given a small daily supply of rice, cornmeal, and butter along with some salt and molasses. If the slaves had a garden, they might also enjoy a few vegetables.

Slaves were never allowed to forget that they were property to be controlled by the master. They could be physically abused and sold. Carolina colonist Francis Le Jau commented that slave owners could *"hamstring, maim and unlimb those poor Creatures for small faults."* Advertisements for runaway slaves included the gruesome details of brands or scars caused by whippings and other tortures inflicted upon them by their masters. These markings could help identify the runaway. The worst punishment slaves could face was being sold away from their friends and families. Some slaves were sold to settle debts or to bring the master a little extra money. Others were sold when their masters retired or died. Some were even sold or given away before they were born. In 1745, for example, Elizabeth Cheesman gave her brother *"the child when it shall be born that my Negro Woman Grace is now with Child with."*

A VERY WEAK PROVINCE

As early as 1708, slaves made up the majority of the population in South Carolina. By 1740, slaves outnumbered whites by two to one. The huge slave population caused fear throughout the colony. White colonists, especially those in the lowcountry, constantly worried that the slaves would band together, rise up, and slaughter them. In 1766, Carolina resident Christopher Gadsden wrote that the colony was *"a very weak Province, and [the] great part of our weakness (though at the same time is part of our riches) consists in having such a number of slaves amongst us."*

The first law to regulate slave behavior in South Carolina was put into place in 1696. That law, the first of many such "slave codes," legally defined slaves as property. Future laws enacted harsh punishments for blacks who ran away, attacked or rebelled against their masters, or otherwise misbehaved.

slave code—a set of laws regulating the behavior of enslaved blacks

Despite these laws, some slaves tried to escape their miserable lives by running away. Between 1732 and 1790, the *South Carolina Gazette* published 602 ads seeking the return of fugitive slaves. In February 1739, for example, Carolina colonist Rebeccah Massey published a notice in the *Gazette* about her runaway slave Ruth. The ad read, *"Whoever takes her up, gives her 50 good Lashes, and delivers her to me, shall have 10£ (about $2,125 today) reward."* Other slaves stood up to their white masters by working slowly or destroying crops or equipment when they could.

Sometimes slaves turned to outright rebellion. In early September 1739, the worst fears of white colonists in South Carolina were realized when a slave named Jemmy led an uprising of enslaved people in Stono, 20 miles (32 km) from Charles Town. A small group of about 20 rebels attacked a warehouse of guns and gunpowder, killing two white guards and seizing the weapons inside.

Carrying a banner with the word "Liberty" on it, the slaves headed south, toward Florida. In 1733, the Spanish had promised any escaped slaves freedom in their colony. As they marched, the rebel group swelled to about 100 slaves. They burned buildings and killed 21 whites—both adults and children. One man, a tavern keeper, was spared because he was *"a good man and kind to his Slaves."*

About 12 hours after the rebellion began, a group of armed whites overtook the slaves and defeated them in battle. Several of the rebels were killed during the skirmish. Although the rest fled, most of them were soon captured. The rebellious slaves were shot or hanged.

The revolt was the largest and deadliest in the history of colonial America. In 1740, Carolina colonists responded by passing a set of harsh new laws known as the Negro Act. Under the act, slaves were no longer allowed to work for themselves on Sundays and were not permitted to gather in groups. Slaves were legally prohibited from learning to read, because colonists believed that literacy would promote rebellion. One part of the act made the murder of a slave by a white person a minor offense, punishable only by a fine. Another section offered rewards to those who brought officials the scalps of runaway slaves. These new laws would remain in effect for nearly 100 years.

CHAPTER SEVEN

Life on the Coast, Life in the Country

SOUTH CAROLINA COLONISTS *drive the Cherokee from the colony in a war that lasts two years. South Carolina's backcountry becomes home to new immigrants from Europe and the northern colonies.*

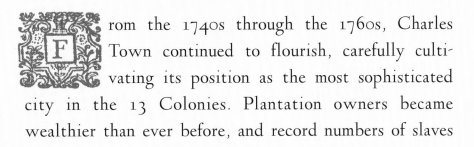

F rom the 1740s through the 1760s, Charles Town continued to flourish, carefully cultivating its position as the most sophisticated city in the 13 Colonies. Plantation owners became wealthier than ever before, and record numbers of slaves

OPPOSITE: A view of Charles Town from the harbor at the intersection of the Cooper and Ashley Rivers. Brisk trade in indigo, rice, and slaves made the port one of the busiest in the Colonies.

were brought into the colony to work on rice and other plantations. Between 1750 and 1775, about 58,000 enslaved people were brought to the colony through Charles Town. By 1770, blacks outnumbered whites in the lowcountry by three and a half to one.

Colonial officials continued to work to convince white settlers to migrate to South Carolina from Europe. They were not very successful. By this time, plantation owners had taken the best land in the colony for themselves.

Framed by a moss-draped live oak, slaves clear land along the Ashley River. These enormous trees have become a symbol of southern plantation life.

The few small settlements already established on the Carolina frontier prospered during the 1740s and 1750s. The Welsh settlers who had made their homes on the Pee Dee River, for example, had encouraged their friends and family members from Wales to migrate to the colony. The Welsh Tract, as their township was known, soon became wealthy by growing indigo crops. The Welsh Tract was one of the few backcountry regions that relied on slave labor. As a result, Welsh Tract settlers more readily associated themselves with the lowcountry plantation owners than with backcountry farmers.

An Ode to Charles Town

In 1769, a Captain Martin gave his impression of Charles Town, a view probably shared by many:

Black and white all mix'd together,
Inconstant, strange, unhealthful weather
Burning heat and chilling cold
Dangerous both to young and old
Boisterous winds and heavy rains
Fevers and rhumatic pains
Agues [fever with chills] plenty without doubt
Sores, boils, the prickling heat and gout [swelling of the joints]
Musquitos on the skin make blotches
Centipedes and large cock-roaches
Frightful creatures in the waters
Porpoises, sharks and aligators
Houses built on barren land
No lamps or lights, but streets of sand
Pleasant walks, if you can find 'em
Scandalous tongues, if any mind 'em
The markets dear and little money
Large potatoes, sweet as honey
Water bad, past all drinking
Men and women without thinking
Every thing at a high price
But rum, hominy and rice . . .
Many a bargain, if you strike it,
This is Charles-town, how do you like it?

THE CHEROKEE WAR

Even in the middle 1700s, the Cherokee deterred many people from settling the South Carolina interior. As white colonists encroached on native lands during this time, relations between the two groups became strained. Although the Cherokee had signed a treaty with Britain, many colonists believed that the tribe was in league with their French enemies.

In 1753, South Carolina governor James Glen built Fort Prince George on the Keowee River to protect the Cherokee from the raids of northern tribes. Two years later, Glen convinced a Cherokee chief named Old Hop to cede most of the tribe's land rights in the colony to Britain. In return, Glen constructed another fortress, Fort Loudoun, to protect the Cherokee against enemy tribes.

In 1759, a group of Cherokee set off to fight the French and Shawnee in Ohio as allies of the English in the French and Indian War. On their way home, the starving warriors slaughtered a cow belonging to a Virginia farmer. Virginia colonists retaliated by killing the Indians and selling their scalps. Infuriated Cherokee began raiding colonial settlements in South Carolina, killing some colonists. Although Carolina's new governor, William Henry Lyttleton, was able to make a short-lived peace, the Cherokee War began in earnest in January 1760.

The Cherokee War lasted for two years, with both sides committing terrible acts of violence and bloodshed against each other. The colonists appealed to Britain for help and were sent a force of about 1,200 Scottish soldiers. By 1761, the Cherokee had been driven into the mountains to starve. The Indians were forced to beg colonial officials for a peace treaty. Under the terms of the treaty, the Cherokee gave up most of their rights in South Carolina. During the American Revolution, the Cherokee would side with the British, hoping to gain back some of their lost territory and power.

Native Americans, pushed off their lands by increasing numbers of settlers, attack livestock on a South Carolina farm, as angry colonists try to drive them away with their guns.

NEW ARRIVALS

Once the most serious danger from the Cherokees had passed, colonial officials again worked to entice settlers to South Carolina's backcountry. Expanding the presence of colonists in the region would keep the Natives from reclaiming land and a large population would aid the econommy of the colony. In 1761, the assembly approved paying for the passage of *"respectable poor Protestants"* from England and Ireland. They also offered these settlers a bounty, raised by taxing anyone who owned slaves. The bounty would help the newest colonists get started in South Carolina.

In the coming years, settlers arrived from Scotland, England, Ireland, Wales (all of which were part of Great Britain), and Germany. Groups of Scotch-Irish settlers who had settled in Pennsylvania, Virginia, and Maryland migrated to South Carolina along with some Germans. In 1764, 300 French Huguenots were given land and the tools needed to produce silk and wine. Although neither of mulberry trees or grapes flourished, the Huguenots remained, turning to other crops.

By 1770, about 30,000 new arrivals from overseas and the more northern colonies had settled in the South Carolina backcountry. Most of these people were poor Protestants, with very few possessions. They came with a few clothes, some pots, pans, and other cooking tools, and a quilt for warmth at night. Men carried an axe and often a rifle. Some settlers brought along a cow and a horse, if they had one.

The backcountry settlers were mostly subsistence farmers, growing food to feed themselves and their families. Others were ranchers, allowing their cattle and hogs to roam through the pine forests and swamplands of the interior. Later, as roads were improved into the backcountry, these colonists would send beef, cheese, butter, leather, and bacon to Charles Town for sale in the markets there.

The homes of the Carolina frontier settlers were very modest. The poorest arrivals started off with a house made from mud bricks or a lean-to until a sturdier log cabin home could be built. Log cabins were small, usually just two rooms with a dirt floor. A single fireplace was used for cooking and heating. Furniture might include a bed, a table, and a few rough chairs.

Backcountry settler Robert Witherspoon recorded his memories of his move from Scotland to South Carolina in 1734:

> My mother and us children were still in expectation that we were coming to an agreeable place, but when we arrived we saw nothing but a wilderness and instead of a fine timbered house, nothing but a very mean dirt house, our spirits quite sunk. . . .
> Evening comeing on, the wolves began to howl on all sides, we then feared being devoured by wild beasts, having neither gun nor dog, nor any door to our house.

CHARLES WOODMASON,
Anglican Zealot

THE MEN AND WOMEN OF THE SOUTH CAROLINA BACKCOUNTRY practiced various religions. There were Scottish Presbyterians, French Calvinists, German Lutherans, and Welsh Baptists. There were, however, few Anglicans in the backcountry.

In 1761, Anglican minister Charles Woodmason set out to change that. He traveled into the backcountry in an effort to convert the frontier Protestants to Anglicanism, the colony's official religion. Woodmason was disgusted with what he found. In 1768, he included the following entry in his diary:

Most of these People had never before seen a Minister, or heard the Lords Prayer, Service or Sermon in their Days. I was a Great Curiosity to them —And they were as great Oddities to me. After Service they went to Revelling Drinking Singing Dancing . . . —and most of the Company were drunk before I quitted the Spot — They were as rude in their Manners as the Common Savages, and hardly a degree removed from them. Their Dresses almost as loose and Naked as the Indians, and differing in Nothing save Complexion —I could not conceive from whence this vast Body could swarm —But this Country contains ten times the Number of Persons beyond my Apprehension.

Men, women, and children worked hard to forge a good life in the wilderness. Unable to afford slaves or servants, the women cooked, helped grow food crops, tended animals, and spun wool into yarn or thread for cloth. Children were kept busy from a young age, learning to help with small chores that grew more difficult as they grew older. With very few schools in the backcountry, children learned only what their own parents could teach them, usually reading, writing, and simple math.

This hand-colored woodcut offers a glimpse into the lifestyle of Carolina backcountry settlers. They lived in log cabins they built from trees they cleared, dug wells for water, grew their own food, and were constantly on the alert for attack by wild animals.

A COLONY DIVIDED

In the 1760s, the backcountry and the lowcountry were two very different places with very different needs. Settlers in the backcountry needed better, wider roads for their wagons so they could take their goods to Charles Town for sale. They wanted better defenses against hostile natives on the frontier.

One of the chief points of contention was the lack of law enforcement and justice in the backcountry. Frontier settlers were at the mercy of gangs of thieves and outlaws who assaulted them, stole their livestock, and destroyed their crops. The assembly in Charles Town, however, refused to fund any constables for the frontier. There were also no courts in the backcountry, which meant that settlers had to travel to Charles Town to record wills, deeds, and other legal documents. All court cases also had to be tried in Charles Town.

constable—officials who maintain law and order

Colonial officials ignored the pleas and demands of the frontier settlers. The assembly was dominated by men from the lowcountry, and they had only their own interests in mind when making laws and dispersing funds. These wealthy men looked down upon the less sophisticated men and women of the frontier. Eliza Pinckney expressed their elitist views when she wrote that *"the poorer sort are the most* indent people in the world or they could never be so wretched in so plentiful a countryside as this."

   In 1769, the assembly finally agreed to establish courts throughout South Carolina. By November, the king had approved the creation of seven court districts, with the court meeting three times a year in Charles Town and twice a year in six districts, which included Beaufort, Georgetown, and Orangeburg. Backcountry colonists were also awarded more representation in the assembly. By the start of the Revolution, the frontier settlements were represented by three delegates in the assembly. ✷

Supporting Revolution

SOUTH CAROLINA JOINS THE MOVEMENT *for independence,
but a Loyalist stronghold remains within the colony leading
to conflict with Patriots. Charles Town is taken by the
British in 1780, but with an American victory,
it is reclaimed by South Carolinians in 1782.*

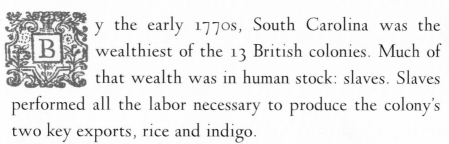 y the early 1770s, South Carolina was the wealthiest of the 13 British colonies. Much of that wealth was in human stock: slaves. Slaves performed all the labor necessary to produce the colony's two key exports, rice and indigo.

Despite its success, South Carolina still relied heavily on Great Britain for its safety and success. The colony

OPPOSITE: William Washington, a cousin of George Washington and an officer in the Patriot army, leads his men to victory in the 1781 Battle of Cowpens.

depended upon the British Navy and Army for protection from Spanish and Indian attackers. Carolina merchants also benefited from British trade laws like the Navigation Acts, which allowed direct exports of certain goods from Carolina to southern Europe.

THE CONFLICT WITH BRITAIN

Colonial dissatisfaction with British rule began in the mid-1760s, when Britain passed a series of taxes on goods imported into America. The taxes were part of an effort by Great Britain to recoup some of the money it had spent fighting the French and Indian War in the Colonies. The French and Indian War between Britain and its Native allies and France and its Native allies was a war for control of North American. It was primarily fought in the Ohio and St. Lawrence River Valleys, areas claimed by both the French and English. Britain's victory in this war removed the French presence in mainland North America and benefited the southern colonies by driving them out of the Mississippi Valley and gulf coast region. The long years of fighting, however, had severely depleted the British government's funds.

In 1764, the British Parliament enacted the Sugar Act, which taxed sugar and molasses, two items that were important to South Carolina. The following year, Parliament enacted the Stamp Act, which placed a tax on all legal documents and many printed materials (including newspapers and even playing cards).

Although lowcountry Carolinians prided themselves on their "Englishness," many were enraged by the new laws. Backcountry colonists, on the other hand, were less upset by the taxes. Many of these colonists were subsistence farmers, working hard to support their families. In the coming Revolution, the backcountry would be the heart of the Tory, or Loyalist, movement in the state.

Tory—a person who remained loyal to Great Britain during the Revolution; also known as a Loyalist

Patriot—a colonist who favored independence from Britain

One of the first men to speak out against Britain was Christopher Gadsden, who quickly organized a Sons of Liberty group to oppose the Stamp Act. In 1765, he was one of South Carolina's delegates to the Stamp Act Congress in New York, where he earned a name for himself as a true Patriot. He impressed other delegates to the north when he said, *"We stand upon the broad common ground of natural rights.... There ought to be no New England man, no New Yorker, known on the continent, but all of us Americans."*

Christopher Gadsden, founder of South Carolina's Sons of Liberty, became a colonel in the South Carolina militia and took charge of the state's military after the war.

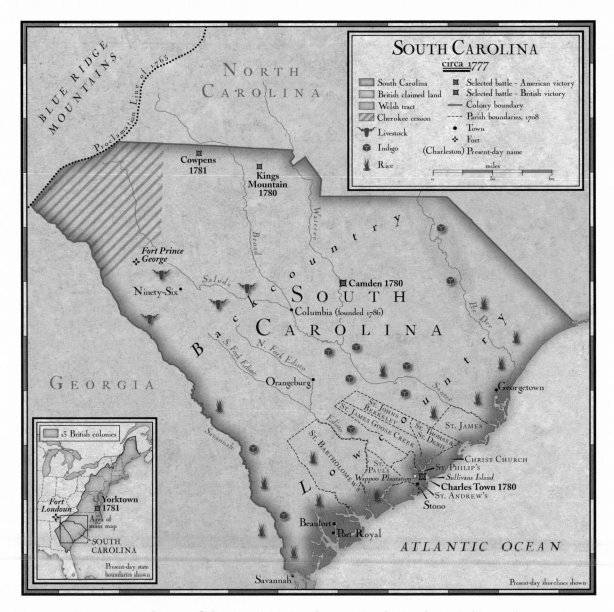

SOUTH CAROLINA
circa 1777

South Carolina	■ Selected battle - American victory
British claimed land	■ Selected battle - British victory
Welsh tract	— Colony boundary
Cherokee cession	- - Parish boundaries, 1708
Livestock	• Town
Indigo	✦ Fort
Rice	(Charleston) Present-day name

miles
0   30   60

BLUE RIDGE MOUNTAINS

Proclamation Line of 1763

NORTH CAROLINA

Cowpens 1781

Kings Mountain 1780

Fort Prince George

Ninety-Six •

Saluda

Broad

Wateree

B a c k c o u n t r y

■ Camden 1780

S O U T H

• Columbia (founded 1786)

C A R O L I N A

Pe Dee

GEORGIA

S. Fork Edisto

N. Fork Edisto

Orangeburg •

Santee

• Georgetown

13 British colonies

St. Bartholomew's

Edisto

St. Johns Berkeley

St. James Goose Creek

St. Thomas & St. Denis

St. James

Fort Loudoun

Yorktown 1781

Area of main map

SOUTH CAROLINA

Present-day state boundaries shown

Savannah

St. Paul's

Wappoo Plantation

L o w

Christ Church

St. Philip's

Sullivans Island

Charles Town 1780

St. Andrew's

Stono

Beaufort •

• Port Royal

Savannah •

ATLANTIC OCEAN

Present-day shorelines shown

By 1775, on the eve of the American Revolution, South Carolina's indigo and rice plantations had made it the wealthiest of Britain's American colonies. Although most of these plantations were in the lowcountry, the Welsh Tract also raised indigo. The Revolution came late to South Carolina. The British victory at Charles Town was short-lived. Patriot triumphs in the backcountry at Kings Mountain and Cowpens drove the British to Yorktown and final defeat.

Later, Gadsden organized boycotts of British goods and served as a lieutenant colonel in the Continental Army.

Continental Army— the troops who fought for American independence during the Revolution under the command of General George Washington

Continental Congress—the law-making body of the 13 Colonies during the American Revolution

By the 1770s, new British laws and taxes had further angered people throughout the 13 Colonies. It became clear that a break between Britain and America was imminent. In 1774, South Carolina sent five delegates, including Gadsden, to the First Continental Congress in Philadelphia. All five signed the document drawn up in the Congress to boycott imports from and exports to Britain—but not before bullying the rest of the delegates into exempting rice from the boycott.

In early 1775, South Carolina took its own steps toward independence. On January 11, colonists formed a provincial congress to take over governance of the colony. Henry Laurens, a wealthy merchant and planter, was named the congress's first president. By September, the last royal governor of the colony, Lord William Campbell, was gone, having fled to the safety of a British warship.

THE REVOLUTION BEGINS

After years of tension and strained relations, the American Revolution began on April 19, 1775. On that day, British soldiers and colonial minutemen battled at Lexington and

Concord in Massachusetts. When news of the battles reached South Carolina in May, the provincial congress authorized the enlistment and training of 1,500 troops.

Patriots in the lowcountry founded an association for blacklisting and punishing supporters of the king. Some Loyalists were driven out of Charles Town. Others were tarred and feathered. One man was hanged after he was found bringing messages to the British on Sullivan's Island.

One of the first battles in South Carolina occurred in November 1775 near Ninety Six, a settlement in the backcountry. The battle was not between the British and the colonists, but between Patriots and Tories. The bloodshed was minimal, but the two-day battle was a warning of things to come. Throughout the Revolution, South Carolina would be torn apart by a civil war between colonists who fought for independence and those who remained loyal to Britain.

THE WAR IN THE SOUTH

During the Revolution, Charles Town was quickly identified by the British as an important target. The port city was an entry point for supplies and ammunition for the rebels. Additionally, the British believed that the large Tory population of Georgia and the Carolinas would rally to their support once Carolina's capital was conquered.

PAYING THE PRICE FOR LOYALTY

In 1775, Dr. George Milligan, a well-respected physician and member of the Charles Town Library Society, suddenly became the target of hatred for his Tory sentiments. When Milligan refused to sign an oath of allegiance to the new Patriot government, he quickly learned that his loyalty to the king could cost him dearly:

I saw them [the Mob] coming towards me, but as I expected no insult, I continued in my seat; . . . I was immediately surrounded by a vast crowd, three or four hundred snakes, hissing, threatening, and abusing me. . . . About a dozen advanced towards me. I put my hand to my sword and they stopt. At this instant my wife . . . ran up to me, flew into my arms and fainted away. . . . I took my wife in my arms and carried her through the Mob, they gave away to us, but closed behind, still threatening me, with some difficulty I got into my house by pushing away those that pressed most upon me. . . . The greatest number of this Mob were the new soldiers at the barracks and mobbing is the only service they will ever be fit for.

Milligan and his family soon left Charles Town.

In June 1776, the British waged their first attack on Charles Town. During the Battle of Sullivan's Island, Patriot commander William Moultrie managed to defeat a superior British force. After the battle, the island's fortress was renamed Fort Moultrie. The British would not attempt another full-scale assault on Charles Town until 1779.

One Patriot who got his revolutionary start at the Battle of Sullivan's Island was Francis Marion, known as the Swamp Fox. Marion, born in South Carolina in 1732, was a Huguenot planter and Indian fighter. He joined Moultrie's regiment at the start of the war. Later, Marion would become famous for his guerrilla tactics against the British, disappearing into the swamps after each attack.

Francis Marion, the "Swamp Fox," and his men ambush British troops in South Carolina before taking cover in a nearby swamp to plan another sneak attack.

In 1778, the British once again turned their attention to the southern colonies. With its small population and strong Tory base, the South was believed to be the weakest and most loyal region in America. The British planned to seize control of Savannah, in Georgia, and Charles Town and make their way north. They hoped that scores of Loyalists and fleeing slaves would help them fight the rebels.

In December 1778, the British conquered Savannah. Throughout 1779, they launched attacks on Charles Town and other towns in Georgia and South Carolina. In April 1780, they finally marched to within a few miles of Charles Town. They laid siege to the capital, digging battle trenches and inching closer day by day. On May 9, British general Sir Henry Clinton gave his soldiers the order to open fire on the town. The wooden buildings caught fire during the attack, and Charles Town's citizens were forced to surrender.

On June 1, Clinton issued a proclamation promising a pardon to those who promised to support Britain and its king, George III. It read, in part: "We . . . do declare, to such of his deluded subjects, as have been perverted from their duty by the factious arts of self-interested and ambitious men, that they will still be received with mercy and forgiveness, if they immediately return to their allegiance."

Despite the offer, far fewer white colonists pledged to support the king than the British had expected. However, hundreds of blacks took the opportunity to escape a life of slavery. Throughout the war, thousands of runaway slaves sought safety and freedom with the British. While some were given arms and allowed to fight, most were set to menial tasks such as digging ditches.

A CIVIL WAR

Many of the battles in South Carolina were between Tories and Patriots in the backcountry. The summer of 1780, after the British took Charles Town and defeated the rebels at Camden in August, saw the worst violence between colonists. General Nathanael Greene wrote, "*The whigs [Patriots] and tories pursue one another with the most relentless fury killing and destroying each other whenever they meet. Indeed a great part of this country is already laid waste and is in the utmost danger of becoming a desert.*"

The attack on Fort Sullivan in Charles Town harbor on June 28, 1776, was a victory for the Americans. The fort was renamed Fort Moultrie for Colonel William Moultrie, who oversaw its construction and defense.

In the autumn of 1780, however, the tide of the war began to turn. On October 7, Patriot forces defeated a Tory force of 1,200 at Kings Mountain. On January 17 of the following year, Patriot troops under Daniel Morgan beat British soldiers at Cowpens. After this defeat, British leaders decided to focus their efforts to the north, where they were eventually defeated at Yorktown, in Virginia. That battle marked the end of the American Revolution.

By December 1782, the defeated British had completely evacuated Charles Town. In celebration, South Carolinians officially renamed the town Charleston.

South Carolina now turned to the task of recovering from the war. Farming and trading in the backcountry quickly returned to prewar levels, but Charleston and the lowcountry plantations had suffered more damage. About 25,000 slaves were missing. Some 5,000 had sailed with the British out of Charles Town. Others had escaped to Florida or died.

In 1786, Columbia, a former trading post located in the center of the state, was chosen as South Carolina's new capital. The move was intended to ease tensions between lowcountry and backcountry residents. On May 23, 1788, South Carolina ratified, or approved, the U.S. Constitution and became the eighth U.S. state. In the coming years, the state, under the plantation system, would thrive, but its prosperity would eventually lead it into a devastating civil war. ❈

TIME LINE

1521   Spanish trader Francisco Gordillo becomes the first European to explore the South Carolina region.

1539   Spanish conquistador Hernando de Soto leaves Florida on an expedition that will take him into northwestern South Carolina.

1562   French naval officer Jean Ribault founds Charlesfort on Parris Island.

1566   Pedro Menéndez de Avilés founds a Spanish settlement, Santa Elena, on the southern end of Parris Island.

1629   Charles I of England grants the Province of Carolana to a nobleman named Robert Heath.

1663   Charles II of England awards a charter for Carolina to eight noblemen, known as the proprietors.

1669   Lord Earl of Shaftesbury and John Locke write the Fundamental Constitutions of Carolina.

1670   The first colonists from England arrive at Port Royal in Carolina.

1671   Colonists arrive in Carolina from Barbados, bringing the first African slaves into the colony.

1680   Charles Town, Carolina's first permanent settlement, is established at Oyster Point.

c.1685   The first rice crops are planted in Carolina.

1685   Groups of French Huguenots migrate to Carolina and other English colonies.

1696   The first slave code in South Carolina is passed.

1700   A serious hurricane devastates Charles Town.

1712   Carolina is separated into two colonies, South Carolina and North Carolina.

1715   The Yamassee War begins.

1719   Colonists rebel against proprietary rule.

1729   South Carolina becomes a royal colony, and the first royal governor arrives.

1732   Georgia is founded, providing a buffer for Carolina against Spanish attack.

1739   As many as 100 slaves rise up during the Stono Rebellion, killing 21 people and burning buildings.

1740   Harsh new laws known as the Negro Act are passed as a result of the Stono Rebellion.

1755   Governor James Glen convinces a Cherokee chief named Old Hop to cede a large chunk of Cherokee land to the colonists.

1760   The Cherokee War begins.

1765   The British Parliament passes the Stamp Act.

1774   South Carolina sends five representatives to the First Continental Congress in Philadelphia, Pennsylvania.

1775   Battles at Lexington and Concord in Massachusetts mark the start of the American Revolution.

1776   In June, British troops attack but fail to capture Charles Town.

1780   In May, British troops capture Charles Town. In October, Patriot forces defeat Tory and British soldiers at Kings Mountain.

1781   On January 17, Patriot troops defeat British soldiers at Cowpens. Nine months later, British general Lord Cornwallis surrenders to General George Washington at Yorktown, Virginia, ending the Revolutionary War.

1782   British troops evacuate Charles Town.

1786   Columbia is chosen as the new capital of South Carolina.

1788   On May 23, South Carolina officials ratify the U.S. Constitution, and South Carolina becomes the eighth U.S. state.

RESOURCES

BOOKS

Earle, Alice Morse. *Child Life in Colonial Days.* Whitefish, Mont.: Kessinger Publishing, 2004.

Levine, Michelle. *The Cherokees.* Minneapolis, Minn.: Lerner Publications, 2006.

Miller, Brandon Marie. *Declaring Independence: Life During the American Revolution.* Minneapolis, Minn.: Lerner Publications, 2005.

* Olwell, Robert. *Masters, Slaves, and Subjects: The Culture of Power in the South Carolina Low Country, 1740–1790.* Ithaca, N.Y.: Cornell University Press, 1998.

Wood, Peter H. *Strange New Land: Africans in Colonial America.* New York: Oxford University Press, 2003.

* College-level source

WEB SITES

African American Heritage
http://www.state.sc.us/scdah/afamer/hpaaheritage.htm Web page hosted by South Carolina's African American Heritage Commission, with links and history

Charlesfort History
http://www.cas.sc.edu/sciaa/staff/depratterc/newweb.htm An archaeological history of the earliest French and Spanish settlements in South Carolina

Cherokee History
http://www.tolatsga.org/Cherokee1.html A history of the Cherokee people in the United States

The National Archives Experience
http://www.archives.gov/national-archives-experience/charters/constitution_founding_fathers_south_carolina.html Brief biographies of the Founders from South Carolina

QUOTE SOURCES

CHAPTER ONE

p. 15 "to the extent...[destruction]." Clowse, Converse D. *Economic Beginnings in Colonial South Carolina, 1670–1730*. Columbia, South: University of South Cartolina Press, 1971, p.37; p. 18 "the greatest...of the world." http://memory.loc.gov/cgi-bin/ampage? collId=gcfr&fileName=0018//gcfr0018.db &recNum=201&itemLink=r%3Fintldl%2F ascfrbib%3A@field%28NUMBER%2B@od1% 28gcfr%2B0018_0177%29%29&link Text=0; p. 19 "It is one...other places." http://memory.loc.gov/cgi-bin/ampage? collId=gcfr&fileName=0018//gcfr0018.db &recNum=201&itemLink=r%3Fintldl%2 Fascfrbib%3A@field%28NUMBER%2B@ od1%28gcfr%2B00180_177 %29%29&link Text=0; p. 20 "cast them...to you possible." http://www.americanheritage.com/articles/ magazine/ah/1963/6/1963_6_8.shtml; "I think it...another in ten." Wright, Louis B. *South Carolina: A History*. New York: W.W. Norton & Company, 1976. p.35.

CHAPTER TWO

p. 24 "true and...Lords Proprietors" http://www.yale.edu/lawweb/avalon/states/ nc01.htm; p. 26 "The land is...our own terms." Greene, Jack P., Rosemary Brana-Shute, and Randy J. Sparks. *Money, Trade, and Power: The Evolution of Colonial South Carolina's Plantation Society*. Columbia, SC: University of South Carolina Press, 2001. p.4; p. 28 "If any maid...for their wives." Salley, Alexander S. *Narratives of Early Carolina, 1650–1708*. New York: Charles Scribner's Sons, 1911. p.73; p. 29 "soe plaine &...bowling alley." Olwell, Robert. *Masters, Slaves, and Subjects: The Culture of Power in the South Carolina Low Country, 1740–1790*. Ithaca, NY: Cornell University Press, 1998. p.10; pp. 29–30 "The natives...well transported thither." Salley, p.45; p. 30 "Here is a...800 calves." ??; "brought deare skins...of the market." Salley, p.117; p. 32 "Noe person...for every child." Shatzman, Aaron M. *Servants into Planters: The Origin of an American Image, Land Acquisition and Status Mobility in Seventeenth Century South Carolina*. New York: Garland Publishing, Inc., 1989, pp. 16–17; "Our friends in...and tools." Roper, L.H. *Conceiving Carolina: Proprietors, Planters, and Plots, 1662–1729*. New York: Palgrave Macmillian, 2004. p.47; "Encourage men of...eate upon us." Shatzman, p.23, 87; p. 33 "And in consideration...five pounds more." Shaltzman, p.32.

CHAPTER THREE

p. 36 "the town...built of wood...." Salley, Alexander S. *Narratives of Early Carolina, 1650–1708*. p. 37 "Nor will people...Indians or pyrates." Roper, L.H. *Conceiving Carolina: Proprietors, Planters, and Plots, 1662–1729*. New York: Palgrave Macmillian, 2004. p 38; p. 38 "a most infectious...(fatal illness)." Shatzman, Aaron M. *Servants into Planters: The Origin of an American Image, Land Acquisition and Status Mobility in Seventeenth Century South Carolina*. New York: Garland Publishing, Inc., 1989, p. 95; p. 35 "After our arrival...like a slave." Anzilotti, Cara. *In the Affairs of the World: Women, Patriarchy, and Power in Colonial South Carolina*. Westport, CT: Greenwood Press, 2002. p.20.

CHAPTER FOUR

p. 51 "They [the Dissenters]...will do any." Wallace, David Duncan. *South Carolina: A Short History, 1520–1948*. Columbia, SC: University of South Carolina Press, 1961. p. 72; p. 57 "hold the reins...be known." Wright, Louis B. South Carolina: A History. New York: W.W. Norton & Company, 1976. p. 62.

CHAPTER FIVE

p. 63 "I have the...through much business." Pinckney, Elise, ed. *The Letterbook of Eliza Lucas Pinckney, 1739–1762*. Chapel Hill, NC: University of North Carolina Press, 1972. p. xi; p. 65 "A gentn...a subservient follower." Anzilotti, Cara. *In the Affairs of the World: Women, Patriarchy, and Power in Colonial South Carolina*. Westport, CT: Greenwood Press, 2002, pp. 42–43; p. 66 "The Gentlemen in...of his company." Anzilotti, p.39; "The Greatest...in Nature." Anzilotti, p. 39; "elegantly finished...on the continent." Cohen, Hennig. *The South Carolina Gazette, 1732–1775*. Columbia, SC: University of South Carolina, 1953. p. 111; p. 68 "unhappy Accident." Cohen, p. 237; "I take this...reasonably expected." Cohen, Henning. *The South Carolina Gazette, 1732–1775*. Columbia, South Carolina: University of South Carolina Press, 1953, p. 238; "[She] mangaged...her son in it." Cohen, p. 239; p. 69 "unmannerly, rude,... talking obscenely." Greene, Jack P., Rosemary Brana-Shute, and Randy J. Sparks. *Money, Trade, and Power: The Evolution of Colonial South Carolina's Plantation Society*. Columbia, SC: University of South Carolina Press, 2001, p. 313.

CHAPTER SIX

pp. 72–73 "Let your...but not old...." Slave sales in colonial Charleston. (South Carolina). Kenneth Morgan. *The English Historical Review* v. 113, n. 453 (Sept. 1998): pp. 905; p. 74 "If a work...be imagined." Snavely, Tipton R. *Economic History of the South*. New York: Prentice-Hall, Inc., 1934, p. 94; p. 77 "hamstring, maim...small faults." Anzilotti, Cara. *In the Affairs of the World: Women, Patriarchy, and Power in Colonial South Carolina*. Westport, CT: Greenwood Press, 2002, p. 50; "the child... Child with." Anzilotti, p. 54; p. 78 "a very weak...slaves amongst us." Greene, Jack P., Rosemary Brana-Shute, and Randy J. Sparks. *Money, Trade, and Power: The Evolution of Colonial South Carolina's Plantation Society*. Columbia, SC: University of South Carolina Press, 2001, p. 280; "Whoever takes...reward." Greene, p. 221; p. 79 "a good man...his Slaves." Olwell, Robert. *Masters, Slaves, and Subjects: The Culture of Power in the South Carolina Low Country, 1740–1790*. Ithaca, NY: Cornell University Press, 1998.

CHAPTER SEVEN

p. 83 "Black and white...you like it?" Merrens, H. Roy, ed. *The South Carolina Scene: Contemporary Views, 1697–1774*. Columbia, SC: University of South Carolina Press, 1977. pp. 230–231; p. 86 "respectable poor Protestants" Wright, Louis B. South Carolina: A History. New York: W.W. Norton & Company, 1976. p. 93; p. 87 "My mother and...our house." Merrens, p. 126; p. 88 "Most of these...my Apprehension." http://www.historymatters.gmu.edu/d/6386/; pp. 90–91 "the poorer sort...countryside as this." Anzilotti, Cara. *In the Affairs of the World: Women, Patriarchy, and Power in Colonial South Carolina*. Westport, CT: Greenwood Press, 2002, p. 18.

CHAPTER EIGHT

p. 95 "We stand...us Americans." Kraus, Michael. *Intercolonial Aspects of American Culture on the Eve of the Revolution*. New York: Columbia University Press. 1928, pp.225–226; p. 99 "I saw them...be fit for." Milling, Chapman J. *Colonial South Carolina: Two Contemporary Descriptions*. Columbia, SC: University of South Carolina Press, 1951. pp.xx–xxi; p. 101 "We...do declare...their allegiance." http://memory.loc.gov; p. 102 "The whigs...becoming a desert." Johnson, George Lloyd, Jr. *The Frontier in the Colonial South: South Carolina Backcountry, 1736–1800*. Westport, CT: Greenwood Press, 1997, p.129.

INDEX

ABOUT THE AUTHOR
AND CONSULTANT

ROBIN DOAK is a writer of fiction and nonfiction books for children, ranging from elementary to high school levels. Subjects she has written about include American immigration, the 50 states, American presidents, and U.S. geography. Doak is a former editor of Weekly Reader and has also written numerous support guides for educators. She holds a Bachelor of Arts degree in English, with an emphasis on journalism, from the University of Connecticut and lives near her alma mater in Portland. She is also the author of *Voices from Colonial America: New Jersey, Georgia, California,* and *Maryland*.

ROBERT OLWELL is an Associate Professor of History at the University of Texas at Austin. He is the author or editor of several books, including *Masters, Slaves, and Subjects: The Culture of Power in the South Carolina Low Country, 1740–1790,* and *Cultures and Identities in Colonial British America* as well as numerous articles on the subject of American colonial history. He has graduate degrees from the University of Wisconsin-Milwaukee and the Johns Hopkins University and lives in Austin, Texas. Olwell is also the consultant for two other books in the *Voices from Colonial America* series: *Florida* and *Georgia*.

ILLUSTRATION CREDITS

NORTH AMERICA Divided into its III PRINCIPALL PARTS 1re ENGLISH Part Viz ENGLISH EMPIRE containi

N Foundland N Scotland N England N York N Jarsey Pensylvania Maryland Virginia Carolina Carolania or Florida California, Sommer Ir Bahama Ir Jamaica &c CARIBY Ir II SPANISH P. viz N.

1685

BAFFINS BAY

ARCTIC

NEW NORTH WALES

NEW SOUTH WALES

HUDS B

L. Piscoutagami

NEW

LAKE SUPERIOR

LAKE HURONS

LAKE ILINOIS

LAKE ERIE

PENN

MAR

I RG

Tract of Land full of Wild Bulls

NEW ALBION

NEW

NEW MEXICO

NEW MEXICO

SEA OF CALIFORNIA

MARAT

NEW BISCAIA

THE GOLF or BAY OF MEXICO

ZACATECAS

CHIAMET

PANUCO

SEA

OF

NEW SPAIN

YUCATAN

HONDURA